Penguin Specials fill a gap. Written by some of today's most exciting and insightful writers, they are short enough to be read in a single sitting – when you're stuck on a train; in your lunch hour; between dinner and bedtime.Specials can provide a thought-provoking opinion, a primer to bring you up to date, or a striking piece of fiction. They are concise, original and affordable.

To browse digital and print Penguin Specials titles, please refer to **www.penguin.com.au/penguinspecials**

ALSO BY ROBERT BICKERS

*Empire Made Me: An Englishman Adrift in
Shanghai*

*The Scramble for China: Foreign Devils in
the Qing Empire, 1832-1914*

Getting Stuck in for Shanghai:

Putting the Kibosh on the Kaiser from the Bund

by

ROBERT BICKERS

PENGUIN BOOKS

Published by the Penguin Group
Penguin Group (Australia)
707 Collins Street, Melbourne, Victoria 3008, Australia
(a division of Penguin Australia Pty Ltd)
Penguin Group (USA) Inc.
375 Hudson Street, New York, New York 10014, USA
Penguin Group (Canada)
90 Eglinton Avenue East, Suite 700, Toronto, Canada ON M4P 2Y3
(a division of Penguin Canada Books Inc.)
Penguin Books Ltd
80 Strand, London WC2R 0RL, England
Penguin Ireland
25 St Stephen's Green, Dublin 2, Ireland
(a division of Penguin Books Ltd)
Penguin Books India Pvt Ltd
11 Community Centre, Panchsheel Park, New Delhi – 110 017, India
Penguin Group (NZ)
67 Apollo Drive, Rosedale, North Shore 0632, New Zealand
(a division of Penguin New Zealand Pty Ltd)
Penguin Books (South Africa) (Pty) Ltd
Rosebank Office Park, Block D, 181 Jan Smuts Avenue, Parktown North,
Johannesburg 2196, South Africa
Penguin (Beijing) Ltd
7F, Tower B, Jiaming Center, 27 East Third Ring Road North, Chaoyang
District, Beijing 100020, China

Penguin Books Ltd, Registered Offices: 80 Strand, London, WC2R 0RL,
England

First published by Penguin Group (Australia) in association with Penguin
(Beijing) Ltd, 2014

Copyright © Robert Bickers, 2014

The moral right of the author has been asserted

penguin.com.cn

ISBN: 9780143800293

CONTENTS

A NOTE ON SOURCES AND TRANSLITERATION

In the endnotes, with the odd exception, I have not referenced individual service or pension files (where these survive), or medal cards (which mostly survive), or fleeting references in the *North China Herald*: there are too many. A more detailed resume of the careers of the *Suwa Maru* contingent will be found online at http://robertbickers.net. The text draws on a close reading of these materials and the Shanghai press, and related sources indicated in the further reading section.

I have generally used the pinyin system of romanisation from Chinese, except where names are more familiar in the older customary style (Peking, Canton, Kuomintang), or simply easier on the tongue (Chapei).

Summer's Lease

The heat set in around 21 June, and for the next forty days and forty nights it stuck resolutely far above the recorded average for the season. Heat stroke took Shanghai bankers and sailors alike into the fraternal peace of the city's cemeteries. Everybody's pace of work slowed. New electric fans and man-powered punkahs delivered what little mercy they could; newspaper adverts touted vitamin tablets to relieve the agony. City businesses still tried to tempt patrons out: the Maxim Garden offered the 'coolest place in Shanghai', open all night for dancing to its Spanish orchestra; the Apollo Theatre promoted the escape of its after-dinner cinema programme and 'cool atmosphere'. If that failed, try hiring a launch for an evening river cruise. But the nights were claustrophobic, and the daytime temperatures simply unrelenting: hour after hour the mercury remained above 32°C.

Then the 'great heat' broke as the Great War broke out, cooling the days and nights, but incubating a fever for violence never before seen, and never to be seen again in Shanghai's clubs, on its riverside Bund and along the Nanjing Road. The city's close to eleven thousand European residents were perplexed and disheartened at the fast-arriving news from Europe, which seemed to threaten everything they had built on the banks of the Huangpu river at Shanghai, and everything they aimed to preserve.

Shanghai's credo was cosmopolitanism, and it was performed all the year round. The city's foreign communities liked nothing better than an excuse for celebration, preferably decorated with the 'Flags! Flags! Flags!' of 'all Nationalities', as advertised by the Santow Yoko store on Boone Road. Even as they sweltered that summer, they were toasting each other and showing off as usual when they marked Independence and Bastille days, and the birthdays of the King and the Japanese emperor. Naval ships were dressed, launched fireworks, and landed men to march and salute. Foreign residents paraded in uniform as members of the Shanghai Volunteer Corps (SVC), and the town band, led by its fine German conductor, Rudolf Buck, played the necessary national hymns and anthems.

On 4 July the Americans had opened up the consulate for Independence Day, with a reception at the

Astor House Hotel, and all Shanghai drank to their liberty. Threading its way through the heat ten days later came the French community, led by the Volunteers carrying lanterns, marching behind Buck's musicians and a *Tricolore*-decorated tram car. At the French consulate and at the elite Shanghai Club it was open house, and the day swam past in toasts of mutual regard. Shanghailanders, as foreign residents called themselves, had nothing but admiration for each other's monarchs and republics, and they pledged friendship and solidarity under the watchful eyes of the crowds of Chinese who lined the streets to watch the parades and the lights. On Bastille Day many of these found themselves learning that the French concession was being extended westward to include their homes. For masked by all this affable cosmopolitanism, and underpinning all of Shanghai's foreign communities, was the practice of empire, of land grabs neatly agreed in treaties, and backed up by warships, garrisons and those marching volunteers.

While the recent anniversary of the 1904 Anglo-French entente was much remarked on in July, Frenchmen and Britons remained wary of each other, and closer and easier relations had long been forged locally between Britons and Germans. They were firm partners in the great Shanghai enterprise. In January Briton Edward Pearce, chairman of the Shanghai

Municipal Council (SMC), had inspected a parade of Germans marking the Kaiser's birthday with a torchlight march. Led by the Mounted Sikhs of the council's police force, and following the band, the SVC German Company marched to the steps of the Club Concordia, the riverside heart of the German community. They were followed by their fellow nationals and 'their friends of other nationalities', and then by marines from the cruiser SMS *Emden*, and a gunboat, SMS *Otter*. Pearce was lavish in his praise: the 'motto in Shanghai was "Omnia Juncta In Uno"', he proclaimed, 'which meant that as they were together collectively, so they all had to pull together'. He was proud that his council could call on the German volunteers, 'who after all were German soldiers, who knew their business and who knew the game'. He was 'more proud than he could say'. All present cried three cheers for the German company, and as they were dismissed the men threw their torches onto a great bonfire on the foreshore.[1]

The Shanghai Municipal Council, comprising nine foreign residents, ran the city's International Settlement. This occupied the heart of the city as it had grown out of the old walled core to the south of the Bund. Sometimes even its British residents mistook it for a British colony, but it was no nation's colony, and while the British predominated, they did not rule. Most of the elected councillors were Britons, but two places were generally

6

reserved for Germans, and by custom one sat as vice-chairman next to Pearce. The British took great care to try to balance their own ambitions with the interests and sensitivities of the others they shared the settlement with. 'Omnia juncta in uno' guided them, though it largely excepted the Chinese, of course.

However, the council's overseas agents were based in London, and procured supplies from Britain, and its several hundred-strong staff was mostly British, and even employed British Indian subjects in the police force. Shanghai was regarded as the capital city of the foreign establishment in China, which stretched north along the coast into Manchuria, west along the great Yangtze river deep into Sichuan province, and south to the very borders of French Indochina. There were scores of foreign-controlled enclaves in the treaty ports – those ports opened to foreign trade and residence since 1842 – but none approached the splendour and the self-regard of the 'Model Settlement' on the banks of the Huangpu.

Since the British had arrived in November 1843, a great city had grown up, spreading west, north and east across the low-lying plain, which was crisscrossed with creeks and streams. The British were joined in their new settlement by other European traders, and neighboured by an American concession, which joined the 'English Ground' to form an 'International Settlement' in 1863. The neighbouring French concession kept its independence. The foreigners at Shanghai built roads, docks, churches and a racecourse; laid out cemeteries and parks, villas and tenements, fine new office blocks, clubs and halls. Their first task had been to raise the waterside embankment, which became their front window, the famous Bund (an Anglo-Indian term). The fine lawns and buildings of the British Consulate General occupied the prime spot on the Bund, and next door on lot No. 1, as was their assumed right, were the stately offices of the 'princely hong', Jardine, Matheson and Company ('hong' meant both a warehouse and a firm). South from there were banks, insurance and trading houses, hotels, newspaper offices and, close by the boundary with the French concession, the Shanghai Club, whose name masked its essentially British character and centrality in British life. Its tree-lined lawns, punctuated with monuments and memorials, were spread along the Bund, topped off with the pleasant Public Gardens in which Buck's musicians played on summer evenings, as Shanghailanders desperately tried to summon sea breezes along the river.

Shanghai's International Settlement housed a polyglot community, with at least thirty nationalities represented – and the category 'British' masked many who came from Canada, Australia and the other English-speaking Dominions. It was far from being simply a community of well-off upper-class expatriate traders working for the great 'hongs' – trading houses like Jardines, or Butterfield & Swire – or the banks. There were certainly enough of those recorded in the regular council census, but foreign residents also worked for the council itself, and for mills and factories, the shipping firms, dockyards, smaller agency houses like Ilberts (whose chairman was Pearce), the Chinese Maritime Customs, the Chinese Post Office, and as salesmen, dairy keepers, tailors, engineers, lawyers, gardeners, hoteliers. Holy Trinity Cathedral employed an organist; there was a golf professional. The council recruited Indian Sikhs for the police force: they were cheaper than Britons, and considered more 'reliable' than Chinese. Hundreds more were employed as private watchmen or supervisors. So the city looked and felt like any one of the transplanted British communities then lodged across the globe. It was distinctive, though, because it was not a colony, and because of its multi-national character, but most importantly because of its relative political autonomy, with power shared between German, American and other interests.

Shipped in with the British were all the social mores of the home country, and then some – for in a smaller community distinction proved generally more important than less. While men in Shanghai thought of themselves as more meritocratic than those back home, or in a British colony like Hong Kong – they had no colonial governor, for example, and ran their own affairs – in reality the strictures and divisions of Edwardian society proved more acute in Shanghai's foreign world. Memoirs and letters remark on this. The *North China Daily News* published a *Ladies Red Book* in which 'calls' – formal social visits – received and made could be recorded, so that Shanghai ladies knew who they could and could not acknowledge socially. You were judged by your clubs, your masonic lodge, your address, your position and your employer, and by your prowess on the sports field. You were also judged by your 'race'. Eurasians – men and women of mixed British-Chinese ancestry, usually British subjects – were generally socially excluded, however prosperous, were routinely discriminated against, and were the subject of public and cultural disdain. It might go without saying that this world almost wholly excluded Chinese from its purview, despite being utterly dependent on collaboration with them.

It was a comparatively comfortable spot to live, even for the working-class Britons of the police force, who were recruited in fairly subordinate roles. Shanghai's British bobbies had a share of a servant – a 'boy' – from the moment of their arrival, who would clean their shoes, fetch shaving water and press their uniforms. Phrasebooks paid particular attention to the directions a 'master' or a 'missee' would need to relay to servants, mostly in 'pidgin' English, some of which bastard lingo foreigners used with each other – chin chin, look-see, maskee (all right), chop chop – for it marked them apart as Shanghailanders. Very few foreigners were required or encouraged by their employers to learn Chinese, and fewer were inclined to. While Shanghai was not cheap, the quality of life was good. You could live a class above your station, and it was a place in which a man or woman might reinvent themselves. Plenty still fell through the cracks, though, and the indigent foreign poor took their share in life or death of their consuls' time.

As the music played in the Public Gardens and amahs tended the children, Shanghailanders reflected on the world, and their world, as revealed in the pages of the *North China Daily News* – 'Impartial Not Neutral' – its competitor, the *Shanghai Mercury*, the American *Shanghai Times*, *Der Ostasiatische Lloyd* – 'Organ Für die deutschen Interessen im Fernen Osten' – or *L'Echo de Chine* – not surprisingly, the 'journal des intérêts français en Extrême-Orient'. Lighter reading came from humorous weeklies like *The Eastern Sketch* or *The Bund*. Closer to local hearts were the green-papered *Sport and Gossip*, and Mrs Mina Shorrock's *Social Shanghai*, in which the local elite could see photographs of itself in all its social pomp and finery.

This lively press, in which new ventures were regularly floated (and just as regularly sank), was augmented with less read learned journals, published by the North China Branch of the Royal Asiatic Society or the China Medical Association, while missionaries read the monthly *Chinese Recorder* to keep up to date with each other and with interminable controversies about, inter alia, the correct Chinese translation of the term 'God'. The press largely represented China to the world, as its editors and contributors doubled as China correspondents for papers abroad, and in many ways it reported the world to China. Local Chinese papers translated its stories, and a growing Anglophone readership read it firsthand.

Reading was all very well, and while cultural pursuits were catered for by Shanghai's active musical and amateur dramatic societies, sport was dearer to many Shanghailanders' hearts. Shanghai shut down twice a year for the races, its foreign business elites competing to run the most successful stables, with young men racing 'China ponies', small sturdy beasts shipped down from Mongolia. The Shanghai Race Club's ground lay in the heart of the settlement, surrounded by housing, where the Nanking Road became Bubbling Well Road. It lay at the centre of local social life, settlement grandees serving on its committees and as stewards and marshals. Within the ground could be found the cricket club and other sports fields, and the press kept its readers happy with detailed reports of the local matches. British

American Tobacco played the Shanghai Cricket Club; the Shanghai Municipal Police played St Andrews. Teams from different treaty ports travelled to play each other. Good shooting was to be had in the canals west of the city, which people navigated on houseboat holidays, while hunters made do with the Shanghai Paper Hunt club (for there were no foxes to chase). The Shanghai Rowing Club held its regattas out north-west at a spot christened 'Hen-li' in honour of the sport's home on the River Thames, and in the summer of 1914 German teams took all the trophies.

The later nineteenth-century European vogue for military volunteering was funnelled into the Shanghai Volunteer Corps, which had been baptised in (mostly friendly) fire at the 1854 'Battle of Muddy Flat'. In the spring it had marked the diamond anniversary of that encounter, and laid the foundation stone of a new drill hall. Britons and Germans were the most enthusiastic volunteers, parading weekly in companies organised by nationality, and wearing their national uniforms, training to defend the settlement from internal or external threats: well, from the Chinese, to be blunt, and they were generally blunt about that. Volunteering or rowing or the paper hunt kept a young man fit and healthy, or at least beat back a hangover, for the settlement's nightlife was already well known.

In its new hotels and in the clubs, and in less salubrious bars and brothels, Shanghai's still overwhelmingly male society enjoyed itself, or sank its sorrows. Recent years had seen a big influx of Eastern European women to work on 'The Line', a street of brothels discreetly lodged behind the British Consulate General, and US officials had grown so concerned at the notoriety of these 'American girls' – as all and sundry knew them – that they had lobbied for a new US court for China to try to clean up America's reputation. This initiative had backfired quite spectacularly – it was not quietly done, and drew much public notice to the American madams and racketeers who helped male Shanghai while away its off-duty hours.

There was plenty more of the seamier side of life, for in the absence of a single jurisdiction each nationality had its own courts and consuls, and perhaps sometimes a consul was not as disinterested as he might have been in the fate of shady enterprises, and might gently obstruct a police investigation. And if one wanted to offer the ever-eager public the opportunity to spin its luck on a roulette wheel at the Jessfield Inn, the Alhambra or Alcazar hotels, then one could provide all sorts of complications and obstructions for the law by having a hotchpotch of nationalities involved in owning, renting, and running the joint. Police frustration could lead to the taking of shortcuts and sometimes violence, as when police chief CD Bruce led Alan Hilton-Johnson and other senior officers to raid the barricaded Jessfield Inn in August 1909. Shots were exchanged, and Police Constable Ernest Engley and three others were fined for assaulting an Indian watchman who had resisted the raid, in a case that seemed for the first time to clarify some of the powers of Shanghai's ambiguously positioned police force.[2]

Most crime was less spectacular. Indeed, racketeering of a sort was a routine part of the day job for many. In 1912 the British consul had concluded that a jury could not be brought together in the settlement to try any man of financial fraud related to the great Shanghai stock exchange 'rubber boom' collapse of 1910.[3] It was not that it was too small a world – there were well over two thousand adult male Britons in the settlement – but that it was such a routinely corrupted one. *Taipans* – managers of the big trading firms – and jobbing small fry alike had set up combines and sold stocks that were, often deliberately, simple engines of fraudulent speculation. The market had been rigged. Shanghai's leading businessmen dabbled in both honest and dishonest business, fronting new breweries to slake the thirsts of the foreign garrisons established after the 1900 Boxer uprising in north China, and setting up rubber companies. Times and laws have changed, and some of what then went on was not illegal, but it was nonetheless routinely viewed as dishonest.

Shanghai was embedded in a network of interests that stretched across China, where over the previous seventy years foreign powers had extracted a bewildering set of differently constituted gains on threat of war, as the price of peace, or simply as compensation for this injury or that, all secured at China's expense. Across the country there was a clutch of foreign-controlled 'concessions' in the hands of eight different powers, as well as formally detached colonies and 'leased territories' snatched by Britain, France, Japan, Russia and Germany. Foreign diplomats declared that they had 'spheres of influence', and demanded first rights to any new gains in those zones, such as railway concessions. Ships from several foreign fleets cruised the coast and the Yangtze and Pearl rivers. At Tianjin eight foreign concessions neighboured each other; at Wuhan there were five. France had detached Indochina from the suzerainty of China's ruling Qing dynasty; Russia had carved off a great chunk of maritime north-east Asia, later fighting and losing a war with Japan over domination of Manchuria, which was largely conducted on Chinese soil. That conflict aside, the powers often cooperated with each other when there was little to be gained through rivalry, though there was still plenty of that. It was no wonder that many Chinese feared 'national extinction', and anger at foreign power and the inability of the Qing to fight it, had contributed in no small measure to the great overthrowing of the dynasty in 1911–12 and the establishment of a new Republic of China.

Foreigners generally welcomed the rise to power of this revolutionary 'Young' China, as they sometimes termed it, and its modernisation plans, as long as it did not disturb their world. This was a forlorn hope, as pushing back against foreign power was fundamental to China's nationalism. But so lost in their own world were the men of Shanghai that they still aimed to expand their settlement. In 1913 Chairman Pearce had authorised an attempted grab of the Chapei district to the north by the police and volunteers – this was when his Germans had done him proud – led by Chief CD Bruce, late colonel in the British army, who commanded both the SVC as well as the police. They had marched in, but had been thwarted and forced to march out again. In 1914 the French were in the midst of their expansion, and the British, having failed by crook, now tried by hook, and began negotiating a formal extension of their concession with the Chinese foreign ministry even as war broke. At their backs, though, they were aware of the rising power in China of Japan, by now a fully-fledged member of the loose consortium of the powers operating in the new republic, although one whose ambitions and interests caused increasing disquiet.

Shanghai's foreigners remained steadfast in their bellicose forward policy, and were committed to defending 'their' city from attack. They kept a watch on the Huangpu, as China's post-revolution order steadily degenerated into regional and factional chaos. In 1913 the Chinese Nationalist Party, the Kuomintang – driven out of the new parliament by assassinations and bribery – had launched a revolt against China's new dictator, Yuan Shikai, and Shanghai was one of the bloody sites of that failed rebellion. The British had helped it fail, by facilitating a loan that kept Yuan's naval forces at Shanghai on his side. They preferred to see a strong man in charge, however much they professed a desire for a democratic China.

The foreigners feared chaos, and they feared revolt. Barely fourteen years earlier the Qing state had joined forces with the anti-foreign Boxers, standard bearers of a massive peasant uprising that swept the north China plain. At Tianjin and at Peking foreign communities had been besieged, and a large multinational force had landed to restore order, and foreign predominance. Tens of thousands died in the immediate conflict and disorder, and then as foreign forces worked their way through rural north China in the winter of 1900–1901 to 'punish' communities deemed to have supported the uprising. As Shanghai sweltered in 1914 its multilingual press reported continuing threats of 'Boxerism' and 'Boxer' bands. Vigilance was paramount.

Such night and press terrors aside, the days before the

Great War were generally fine by the Huangpu. For the Reverend Charles Darwent, author of the settlement's recently published guidebook, *Shanghai: A Handbook for Travellers and Residents*, earth, or certainly Asia, had nothing to show more fair than the varied sights of Shanghai. Its temples and its guildhalls were, as his preface put it, 'much more beautiful and imposing buildings than any in Japan', saving the odd tomb, and Darwent guided his readers to all the best spots to view the city's charms and record them on the cameras he assumed they carried. This strikingly bizarre view – for there was little that was beautiful about Shanghai – shows how partisan supporters of the 'model settlement' could be. They were proud of what they had achieved and had built in China. Shanghai – and they always co-opted the whole of the city into their rhetoric when they talked of their settlement – stood out as the model of all treaty ports. It was the 'mother' of them all, as banners marking its fiftieth anniversary had claimed as early as 1893. The settlement stood proudly as a rebuke and a challenge to the Chinese city authorities, daring them to reform and modernise their city.

Shanghai also stood out, the foreigners felt, as a paragon of modern cosmopolitanism. A memorial to the shipwrecked crew of the German gunboat the *Iltis* stood on Jardine Matheson-owned land at the entrance to the Public Gardens, permission for which was granted 'with much pleasure' by the company. As one missionary writer noted: 'On British ground has been reared a monument painfully precious to the great German Empire.'[4] The Germans of the Club Concordia – opened with great patriotic fanfare in 1907 – had returned such favours. They hosted the British members of the Shanghai Club during the years the Shanghai Club was being rebuilt, so the city's most prominent Britons had enjoyed the hospitality of their German friends in this fine German-styled building, the 'most prominent edifice on the Bund' with 'beautiful mural paintings representing Berlin and Bremen', Vienna and Munich, the rafters in the bar decorated with apt quotations, and its dining room dominated by an impressive portrait of the Kaiser.[5] National pride was assuaged through such patriotic display, but in practice they were all much more pragmatic about the alliances they formed in business and in the chambers of foreign power, and they played, marched, raced, rowed, sang and celebrated together.

In fact many foreigners paid little regard to the fine details of the imperialist politics of the concessions. They might applaud their diplomats for seizing a few acres of yet another Chinese city and raising a flag on it (or damn them for failing to), but they lived and worked where they wanted to, and while they might leap in if the terms looked good, they generally did not feel the need to relocate a business already established in a foreign power's concession, if at last their home government finally caught up with their private-enterprise imperialism and established a new concession for them. Britons lived in German Tianjin; Germans lived in Shanghai's French concession, all higgledy-piggledy. Open the 1 August 1914 *North China Daily News* and take your pick from the Russian, German, Belgian, French, British or Japanese banks, or shipping or insurance firms. Try a glass of Asahi beer or a Tsingtao, sip a King George IV Scotch whiskey, or try some Evian Table Water. It was all laid out for the comfort and delight of China's foreign residents. Ethos and practicality made the business of coming to hate each other in the heat of 1914 not only difficult to fathom, but awkward to enact.

They had had enough prompting, of course, as all Europe had. The pre-1914 barrage of fearmongering in the press and in popular novels had readied the continent for the worst. Since 1871 Anglophone popular culture and public debate had periodically feasted on klaxon tales of German invasions of an 'unprepared' United Kingdom. More recently and alarmingly the *Daily Mail* had employed troupes of German-uniformed sandwich-board men to parade in English towns, advertising its serialisation of William Le Queux's tale *The Invasion of 1910*. Spies were spotted everywhere, lurking in the guise of German waiters, bandsmen and commercial travellers. Copycat pieces and rebuttals had fanned the flames, and German and French writers contributed gleefully to the genre. Everyone loves a fright.

In East Asia colonial Hong Kong had chided itself on its inadequate defences in October 1897, when the *China Mail* serialised a tale of a Russo-French invasion of the island.[6] But in Shanghai the foreigners had looked elsewhere for their enemies, worrying what Chinese forces might do if Europe was plunged into war. Shanghai's own invasion stories saw Chinese forces overwhelm the settlement when the foreign fleets were called away to a Europe newly distracted by internecine warfare.[7] In 1900 these nightmares had seemed to come true, with Britain mired in its South African war and all Europe distracted by it; the Chinese army's new Krupp artillery shelled the concessions at Tianjin, and peasant fighters raided mission stations and railway installations. They were beaten back, but it was a warning to Shanghai to continue its watch.

In 1914, in the last days of sweltering July the telegraph offices delivered incredible telegram after incredible telegram from Europe. Up and down the Bund and in the clubs the men and women of Shanghai gathered to talk as events unfolded after the assassination of Archduke Ferdinand and Austria-Hungary's ultimatum to Serbia. On Tuesday 28 July the consul general of Austria-Hungary had placed the empire's mobilisation order on the front page of the

North China Daily News, and that same day declared war on Serbia. Two days later Russia mobilised. On Saturday 1 August things came to a head: 'rumour was busy all morning'; 'war fever' gripped everyone. People waited at the Reuters office on Nanjing road, or shared the news at their clubs. The Public Gardens were emptier than usual as Buck conducted the afternoon and evening programmes of light popular music. The Swiss community's annual celebrations might have been a little muted, not least as it took the form of a shooting competition at the SVC rifle range. German and British Shanghailanders sailing north from Hong Kong that day 'kept apart and did not speak', reported one of their number, 'from a mutual dread of broaching a dangerous topic'. The small fire that broke out on board mid-journey might have provided some welcome relief.[8]

What should Shanghai people do? For some there was no option. Law required that they rejoin the colours: the German consul general issued its mobilisation order that same baking Saturday, so some of Shanghai's Germans were the first to leave, making their way north to join the garrison at the port of Qingdao, in Germany's leased territory in Shandong province. Twenty men caught the midday Nanjing express train, followed in the evening by another forty, five of Buck's musicians among them. Some of the hysterical enthusiasm for the conflict that was starting to sweep Europe edged in. A crowd of 300 men and women assembled at the station, singing 'Die Wacht am Rhein', and 'Deutschland, Deutschland über Alles'. The reservists were given a tub-thumping speech by the editor of the *Ostasiatische Lloyd*, and then the men trundled north.[9]

As Shanghai slept that first night of August, Europe embraced its war: the French and German governments issued their mobilisation orders, and Germany declared war on Russia. The consuls in Shanghai were part of the chains of command that reached from their capital cities into China, so for them things were clear enough. Regulations flew in as states creaked onto a war footing in the first days of August, as Germany declared war on France and invaded Belgium on the third, and Britain and its empire went to war with Germany the following day. But a consul's writ at Shanghai extended only over people, not over land, and over such moveable property as was registered as British, or German – merchant shipping for example. So as staff at the consulates worked late into the gas-lit night decoding telegrams and preparing official notifications, their new enemies strolled the streets. Sir Everard Fraser, His Britannic Majesty's Consul, had to pass the Club Concordia on his way to *tiffin* at the Shanghai Club. Perhaps he took a back route – somewhat undignified for a man of his position – or crossed over the Bund to the lawns, but there he had to pass the *Iltis* monument, freshly decorated, as likely as not, with a memorial wreath.

German Consul General Hubert Knipping, for his part, had to pass his British counterpart's office on his way south to the Concordia, or else walk by two British memorials, and one of those to the 'Ever Victorious Army', led in its last phase by General Charles George 'Chinese' Gordon, the British Empire's greatest celebrity. Best to avoid that one. It was easier for the French consul, whose concession was a part of the French Empire, so his word there was in fact law, but still, by rote, the next chairman of the municipal council was to be German, and there were over 200 of his peers living in the concession. The consul resigned his seat to keep the local peace.

American journalist John Powell later recalled how Britons and Germans would cut each as they strolled to their respective clubs, but at first they must have found it puzzling, for they were so much a part of each other's business that it seemed impossible to break apart.[10] They founded companies together, and sat side by side on boards of directors and sports club committees. How do you cut such a man, when you still have business to discuss, or family, or racing affairs? One of the directors of the *Shanghai Mercury* was German, and the *Ostasiatische Lloyd* was printed on the *Mercury*'s press. Edward Pearce and banker Heinze

Figge sat on the council together, and Figge chaired the Watch Committee, which oversaw settlement policing and defence, and which employed scores of British ex-servicemen. Buck and his remaining fellow nationals provided the soundtrack to settlement leisure and Public Gardens lounging. The German Company of the SVC was armed with British rifles, and supplied with ammunition by the government of Hong Kong. Some had poured scorn on the war prophets, on William Le Queux and his tribe, arguing that advanced economies were so integrated that war was impossible. Perhaps only in Shanghai did this argument approach realisation, but then only because many Britons and Germans there actively willed it to.

Rally together, the *North China Daily News* pleaded on 4 August, as the dark news from Europe arrived:

> Shanghai, as we are often reminded, is a cosmopolitan place, where, in spite of occasional causes of ill-feeling elsewhere, many nationalities contrive to dwell together in a very friendly spirit. In the days that are coming it is to be feared that this friendliness will be tested as it has never been before.

Glorying in victories far afield could spark trouble here on the Huangpu, Owen Green, the paper's editor wrote:

> We have spoken of Great Britain's heritage in

Shanghai which it is the duty of the British community to conserve. The same may be said of every nation here represented. No greater patriotism can be shown by the different communities gathered in Shanghai than in determining to respect each other's feelings for the common good during the dark days of war.

So Green argued for public cosmopolitan solidarity at least, to preserve imperialism's grip on Shanghai, and the 'heritage' that all shared.[11]

The concern about a Chinese threat was widespread. As Britain mobilised for war, Consul General Everard Fraser immediately wired the legation in Peking, mindful of the real danger the settlement faced. As British naval forces were being withdrawn, might his chief, the British Minister Sir John Jordan – the ambassador – persuade the Americans to detail a warship to fly the foreign flag in the port? There were restless Chinese troops locally, and 'rumours of disturbance in accordance with avowed plan to utilize foreign complications'. It was Fraser's first note to Peking about the war. Later he wrote to ask whether Yangtze River patrolling by all the powers might resume, Germany included (it would tie up their ships), for, although a 'shocking' proposal, it was 'less shocking than any form of local disturbance of unprotected foreigners'.[12] The Shanghai police increased the stores of ammunition held at each station, and the council also immediately set about a recruitment drive for the SVC as increasing numbers of its members resigned to join up, many parlaying their experience in the corps into recommendations for commissions.[13]

Green's call for calm and restraint locally had a ready audience, and not just among the British. 'Here we are, and all of us wish to remain, after the war is over,' wrote one of the enemies, in impeccable English, to the paper in late August. Beware of those 'wildest rumours' that were sweeping the port, and their impact on 'our "hosts" here' – the Chinese, he meant. Briton and German were and would be 'dependent on each other' to preserve their camaraderie and their Shanghai foothold against the manoeuvres of their 'hosts'.[14] The war was considered a duty – even a crusade – by those on both sides. They did not doubt that it was necessary or that it was just. But even so it was a 'complication', locally, and its contradictions bedevilled Shanghailanders for months, indeed for years afterwards. Still, the war called unrelentingly, and so they tumbled out of Shanghai, many of them, hundreds in total, and then off the ships that carried them home, and on, inexorably on, through training grounds and transports and into trenches and fields of combat across the world.

All Aboard the
Suwa Maru

Surely no one could doubt the loyalty of the Shanghai British on the morning of 16 October, when some seven thousand people crowded the Bund and its pontoons and jetties, the rooftops or windows of the nearby buildings, or assembled on boats in the harbour. They had come – Britons, naturally, but others too, especially Japanese, as well as Chinese – to send off the Shanghai British volunteers. These 110 men from all walks of life had arrived to board the harbour tender the *Alexandra*, which would take them out to the Nippon Yusen Kaisha line's new steamer, the SS *Suwa Maru*. As the men gathered at the Customs jetty the crowd prepared its flags and handkerchiefs. Various brass bands struggled for a hearing, but as the *Alexandra* moved off at eight-thirty a.m. there was a 'tremendous cheering and hat waving', firecrackers exploded, launches blew their sirens and cars their horns, and then 'God Save the King' was sung until the tender moved out of view as it headed down river.

Photographs show the cheerful crowds, men, women and children of all nationalities, including 400 uniformed Japanese students holding flags. All seem bemused at their part in the great gathering on the riverside, for it truly was 'a scene unprecedented in the history of Shanghai'. It was also the culmination of a lengthy send-off that had begun with a special service at Holy Trinity Cathedral two days earlier – 'we wish our brethren who are going to the war "God Speed" and a safe return', declared the Reverend Walker – and continued the following day with a soccer match, and then a reception at the modern Palace Hotel on the Bund at the top of the Nanjing Road. 'I wish I was younger,' declared the hotel's owner, seventy-year-old Brodie Clarke, 'but I have lived too long in Shanghai. I have lived long enough, though', he concluded, 'to know that the men of Shanghai, when they put their hearts and minds to a thing, will do it well.'

In the late summer and early autumn Consul General Everard Fraser had begun to grow frustrated with his charges, and chafed at the limitations to his power presented by extraterritoriality and the international character of the settlement. As Shanghai was no colony, he could issue few orders, and needed instead to persuade, exhort and cajole. He reported feeling that his 'word runs a good deal more than it used to', especially with the council, which was in the habit of pressing back against consular 'interference' – unless it needed a good show of force. But all around Fraser were pro-Germans: Chinese officials, Americans, 'renegade' Britons, simple souls adhering to the neutral ethos of the Customs Service, or shadier ones, so wedded to the cosmopolitan ideal – 'extreme cosmopolites' Fraser dubbed them – that they failed in their duties as Britons.[15] Many others, not least the Japanese, he felt, were biding their time. Many of the 'cosmopolites' in turn feared the Japanese more than they feared the Germans, heeding Green's call to remember the 'heritage' the Europeans shared; their concern with a 'white' solidarity in the face of Chinese or Japanese challenges overrode the exigencies of war. Fraser must have been gratified, then, that from early September onwards a steady stream of patriotic young Britons – mainly policemen – came to the consulate to seek advice and assistance in leaving their posts to go and serve.

In Frenchtown 200 reservists had immediately answered the consul's proclamation of war, and its notice asking men to renew their military service. Many Shanghai Britons on leave back home had also rushed to the colours. On 25 September large crowds cheered off thirteen Britons who left on a French steamer, the *Polynesien*. In photographs the volunteers in their summer best look as if they are heading off on holiday. Feted when they stopped there en route by the governor of Saigon, they travelled third class, mostly, reporting in letters back on the novelty of arrangements on board – not a waiter to be seen; they were not men accustomed to slumming it. All aimed to offer themselves to cavalry regiments and they exercised as they went, skipping, ball-throwing and boxing to keep them fit and pass the time on the journey back.[16]

Some prominent figures in China were able to quit their posts for the duration: former settlement police chief Bruce, who had been forced to resign after the Chapei debacle in 1913, and who had taken a post as a Chinese government advisor, took leave, and left for Great Britain in early October, expecting to get a senior command. Bruce had only joined the police in 1907, having served over twenty-five years in the army, most recently raising and leading the Weihaiwei Regiment of Chinese soldiers in Britain's north China territory. A 'personal friend' of Lord Kitchener, the Minister for War, he soon found himself leading the army's 27th Brigade.

The council's staff, however, which included the Shanghai Municipal Police (SMP), formed the largest pool of Britons of military age in Shanghai. But the position of the police was awkward, for they were legally bound by their terms of service. Since 1910 these had been backed up with 'King's Regulations', issued by the

British minister in Peking, which made breaking them a criminal offence. The regulations had been introduced to enforce a military-style discipline over the police force, ensuring its effectiveness, but they now meant that some of the former military men in the force were in a bind. Their experience made them prime candidates to rejoin the armed forces, which in some cases they had only just left for civilian life, but the council could prosecute them if they broke their contracts. Fraser had had to agree that the regulations held greater sway in law than the call to arms.[17] But not all of those affected had been honest with the council about their reserve status when they joined, so some deserted the police anyway.

The council made it clear initially that it would indeed hold its staff to their contracts. Young police cadet Kenneth Morison Bourne, was fresh off the boat and back in Shanghai – where he had been born – after a commission in the South Lancashire Regiment. He applied for leave to rejoin, and was refused. Acting Chief Superintendent of Police Alan Hilton-Johnson also applied for permission to leave on similar grounds. The council's minutes report that the Watch Committee chairman, Heinz Figge, met him to try to persuade him to stick to the police force. In what must have been a surreal meeting, a German banker had tried to persuade a British officer, personally, not to proceed to war. Hilton-Johnson deflected the approach, saying that such an appeal needed to be made to the General Officer Commanding at Hong Kong.[18]

Fraser decided to take matters in hand, for he was not a patient man. German Consul General Knipping thought him a 'great fanatic' who aimed to foment unrest in Shanghai as a pretext for a British takeover. Zealous he certainly was, at the very least. Customs Commissioner FS Unwin, no less loyal a Briton, declared Fraser a 'monomaniac, a super militarist, blind to any British interests except those of His Majesty's fighting forces'.[19] Sir Everard summoned the British councillors to the consulate on 7 October and told them that they must let men leave. Fraser 'dragooned' them, reported Unwin. If they did not agree he would annul the relevant sections of the regulations, and the council would find that no prosecution would succeed. Law needed to make way for war.

The councillors were not happy with this, fearing that with police recruitment now closed off, the force would in time grow more and more inefficient, and Shanghai more insecure, but Fraser had his way. All men with prior military service in the force, some 175 out of the total of almost 270, would be allowed to apply to leave, but allowance was made for the security of the settlement, and a quota of thirty-five was agreed. By the end of the day Fraser had a committee set up to coordinate and fund the enterprise, and special rates agreed with the Nippon Yusen Kaisha (NYK) shipping line.[20]

In early August there had been talk of raising in Shanghai a 'British contingent' to augment the defence of Hong Kong. The British press demurred, arguing, as it did consistently, that Shanghai might need defending first. But a somewhat cryptic advertisement graced the front page of the *North China Daily News* from 8 September onwards: 'WANTED: MEN who can ride and shoot'. At first it indicated that the men should buy their own '(not China) ponies', but then this was dropped. A scheme for a Shanghai mounted contingent was developing. Things gathered steam in early October, and did so fairly rapidly. Sir John Jordan had secured agreement from the War Office in London that it would accept recruits from Shanghai if they made their own way home and that it would repatriate them when the war was over.[21] The China Association, the body representing the interests of British traders, volunteered to organise the payment of fares home for up to 110 men and to coordinate their passage. The men needed to be under thirty-five years old, over five foot six inches tall, and thirty-five and a half inches around the chest. The council advertised its change of policy regarding its staff, and the China Association placed an advertisement in the press announcing its sponsorship, and the places were filled swiftly.

Almost eighty men applied for the thirty-five passages reserved for the municipal police, and others came forward from various branches of the council's service. Recruits came from private companies, too: a group from Jardine Matheson and Co., five men from the tobacco firms, another gang from Standard Oil, and some from the Customs. Young assistants from Shanghai's foreign department stores applied, some freshly arrived in the city, but so too did young men who had been born in China. All were required to be able to ride, and to have had some former military experience – but in some cases a year's service in the volunteer corps was deemed enough (while one man, Arthur Brown, was accepted solely on the basis of serving with the Boy's Brigade). One or two may have embroidered their qualifications out of gung-ho spirit, or because they were angling for a free ride home. Regardless, they were to travel under military conditions, for Captain Hilton-Johnson was to lead the men home, assisted by Kenneth Bourne, and he would do his best to start to make soldiers of them all on the journey to Europe. Most of the firms, as well as the council, agreed to hold the volunteers' posts open for them. The exception was the Customs Service, which regarded the recruits as deserters – for as an agency of a neutral state it could not encourage the departure of volunteers from its ranks (but it did hold open the posts of reservists from both sides who were legally required to rejoin).[22]

Many of the men had only just arrived in Shanghai. Frank Stubbings, Ernest Eva, Charles Phillips, and RW Tear had pitched up in a draft for the Shanghai police on the SS *Nagoya* in June. Ernest Fearn, Alfred Scudamore and Jim Lovell had preceded them by barely three months. Edward Trotman, an 'ideal Customs officer', and George Gilbert, 'a man of character and parts', had arrived in a recent draft from Britain of experienced men recruited from the ranks of the Waterguard.[23] Others had spent up to a decade patrolling Shanghai's streets, often after a few years in the army or Royal Marines. Police Sergeant Michael O'Regan had seen action in the Boer war, as had Harold Smeeton, who had served further afield on the Gold Coast and in British East Africa as a policeman, and who was also a new arrival locally. Draper's son Ernest Engley, one of those convicted after the Jessfield Inn raid, had been out in China for eight years when he signed up. Some had been born in Shanghai, like William Martinson, son of a customs official, or Herbert Cranston, whose engineer father had recently retired back to Scotland after a thirty-year career in the city. Alfred Singer was another recruit; his father had knocked around a fair bit locally, formerly serving in the SMP and in the British concession at Zhenjiang, after arriving on the same ship in Shanghai in 1866 as his son's fellow volunteer Tom Wade's father.[24]

Except for the number of men reasonably fresh from

military service, the volunteers were a fair cross-section of Shanghai's British community and its history. At least one had seen unemployment and a recent appearance for drunk and disorderliness in front of the magistrate.[25] As departure loomed some of them got their teeth fixed, while others drew up their wills, setting their affairs in order; the men were all set. Fraser accompanied them to the ship, gave them a final pep talk, and departed. Then, as the *Suwa Maru* sailed west on its maiden voyage, the men of Shanghai got ready for war.[26]

The whole enterprise quite clearly transgressed China's neutrality regulations, which forbade recruiting by the belligerent nations, but that was not going to stop Sir Everard. All the long way home – the ship took rather more than the advertised forty-one days and did not arrive in Britain until 15 December – the men began the business of becoming soldiers. The ship was a 'trooper', wrote one man back to the *North China Daily News*, so naturally conditions for them were a bit spartan, even if some travelled in comfort. The men bunked in the first hold aft, which was expressly rearranged for them, with berths on all four sides and the centre arranged for meals. Hilton-Johnson divided them into squads of twelve men, and for five hours a day – 'in no half-hearted manner' – had them exercising, learning semaphore signalling and drill. Then he lectured them. Hilton-Johnson had enough experience to furnish his lectures: officer training at Sandhurst had been followed by a commission in the Lincolnshire Regiment, with colonial postings to Malta and Egypt, and action at the Battle of Omdurman in 1898. Transferred to India and then in 1900 to the Weihaiwei Regiment, he led his men into the battle at Tianjin during the Boxer War. He left the Chinese regiment when it was disbanded and joined the SMP, as did many of his Chinese soldiers, who had paraded at the Customs jetty to wish him farewell.[27] So Hilton-Johnson, like many of his peers, had seen action, and he had observed the Russo-Japanese war as well, but the small colonial wars he mostly knew – in which semaphore certainly played a part – were not the war the *Suwa Maru* sailed towards.

Some boxed their way west, while others pursued more unusual fitness methods. 'Personally I have gone in for breathing exercises', wrote one man, and 'put on an inch around the chest', and a stone in weight, building his body up for the fray. The popularity of sport in Shanghai had perhaps been undermined for some by its night-time delights, and many of the men were less fit than they supposed. It was stifling hot, especially in the hold, and some of the ex-soldiers said that it was 'worse than any barrack in England', and a bit more surreal too, for Japanese passengers seemed to monopolise the bathrooms. 'It's a very decent crowd we have on board,' remarked one correspondent; but for some more used to comfortable travelling, it was a bit of a shock. Hilton-Johnson travelled first class, Bourne and Shanghai barrister John Edwards in second, but the rest of them were in the hold. 'I shall get a deck-chair at Hong Kong and make jolly good use of it,' one decided, Shanghailander-fashion. A man who takes a deckchair to war might be thought to have some unpleasant discoveries coming.

The ship spent a few days in Hong Kong, giving the men time for a quick spot of tourism – up to the Peak to enjoy the view, off to the bars – and then sailed on to Singapore and next to Penang, on what many seemed to think was simply a bit of an adventure. All the while the men drilled on the aft main deck, and rehearsed a military discipline, posting guards on board when they hopped off at Hong Kong; the slowly emerging group of 'utter rotters' who proved 'too lazy to attend drill' were shunted into third-class quarters and to Coventry, and the passenger list at London records their arrival separately to the 'Shanghai contingent'. One man took ill at Hong Kong and disembarked (never getting to the war at all thereafter), and two joined there.

At Penang the men met war for real. Dead Russian sailors floated upside down in the harbour, and 'no one seemed to be doing anything about it', Bourne later recalled.[28] The port was in chaos. They had arrived the day after the German cruiser *Emden* – whose marines had marched along the Bund back in January – had dashed through the harbour at dawn and in disguise – 'the colossal cheek of it all!' – had torpedoed the Russian cruiser *Zhemchug* and a French destroyer and then successfully escaped. Before the *Suwa Maru* reached London the *Emden* had been cornered and disabled, but now things got hotter and more fractious on board the ship. The threat posed by the German cruiser wreaked greater havoc to Allied shipping than its guns or torpedoes did, and it held up the *Suwa Maru*'s passage west through the sea of panic that was the Indian Ocean. Wartime censorship in the British colonies meant that the volunteer contingent garnered little press attention at Hong Kong and Singapore, but a clergyman at the latter port rounded up a hundred books for them and seventy-five tins of cigarettes, and a crowd gathered to send the men off and wish them 'a quick entry into Berlin'.[29]

The ship itself was much noticed and admired, and was shown off en route, with refreshments served to prospective passengers in Hong Kong and Singapore. Launched in Nagasaki on 29 March, it was one of three 12 000-tonne steamers built in Japan specifically for the Japan–Europe service. Over 500 feet long, it could take 14 000 tonnes of cargo, 122 first-class passengers, sixty in second, and almost 180 in steerage. It was fully kitted out for modern safety – it had a 'practically unsinkable' design, and for modern comfort, plenty of ventilation and hundreds of fans. There was a barber-shop, a laundry, and even a darkroom. 'Cleanliness' was the 'company's watchword,' and there was plenty of deck space for first-class passengers (cricket nets could even be set up), and a reasonable amount for those travel-ling second.[30] It was a striking example of Japan's rapid arrival on the international scene, and the development of the country's industrial capacity.

But the *Suwa Maru* was not proving the height of com-fort and cleanliness for the British contingent. Despite a swimming pool being erected after leaving Colombo in Ceylon on 16 November, a 'jolly time' was not being had by all. Some roughed it in the military-style steerage as a novelty, but for others it was a familiar passage, if leaner than usual. The £6–10 travelling expenses did not go far. The social divisions that had been subsumed in the hold started to re-emerge: some were so short of cash that they did their comrades' washing – the showcase laundry was expensive – for a penny a piece.

Bourne, impatient to get into uniform, had cashed in his ticket at Penang when the ship was held up, and taken a P&O steamer onwards. The ship was full of planters from Malaya, and receiving on board new volunteers at each stop, nursing hangovers and cheered on board by friends and family. At Malta it encountered the Australian ship HMAS *Sydney*, which by then had wrecked the *Emden*, and at Marseilles the *Suwa Maru* caught up with it. The Japanese liner had steered well clear of Italy, in case the country belatedly joined its former allies Germany and Austria-Hungary, and the discomforts of the trip after leaving Port Said in Egypt – bad weather meant the hold was battened down – were alleviated by a final concert, graced by some of the first-class passengers, who were otherwise wholly insulated from the band of warriors holed up aft. 'After each item we chipped in with "Tipperary" and brought the evening to a close with the National Anthem sung with unmistakeable fervour,' recalled one recruit.

Hilton-Johnson and others headed overland by train from Marseilles, but when the men arrived in London on 15 December their chief was there to meet them – he was 'a real brick', one man reported – together with the chairman of the China Association, and the men marched through London streets to the Central Recruiting Office in Whitehall, and there and then joined up. By the time the contingent had reached London they were ninety-nine strong. The council would sack four of its policemen who had sailed: a couple were suspected of having used the opportunity to get a free passage home; one was found after departure to have been pilfering from a police social fund. The great majority, however, were itching to get to war.

'I felt joyful at being back in London town,' remembered Alfred Grimble later. He was a Lambeth man who had had six years' experience in the Royal Marines after 1900, before joining the Shanghai police. 'Most of the police fellows enlisted in the 10th Yorks,' he recalled, following Hilton-Johnson, 'as at that time the one regiment was as good as another.'[31] The 10th Battalion of the Yorkshire Regiment (the Green Howards) was one of two units – the other was King Edward's Horse – that the men of the Shanghai contingent joined en masse. Hilton-Johnson had secured his own appointment through his former fellow officer in the Weihaiwei Regiment, Wilfrid Harry Dent, who after retiring from the army in 1907 had landed a job in Shanghai, and a great deal of cricket there. On business in India when war was declared, Dent had rushed back and got a post with the Yorkshire Regiment.[32]

From the *Suwa Maru* thirty men joined the 10th Yorks, mostly as privates, although Hilton-Johnson recommended four of the contingent for commissions. Missionary's son William Cornaby and his colleague, Vaughan Craddock, a silk appraiser with Jardines, T. Rowley Evans, an SMC clerk, and Herbert Such, from Hankow, had all passed muster in his eyes, not least socially, on the journey home.[33] Ilbert & Co's Geoffrey A. Turner also secured a commission. These men were clearly able to satisfy the War Office that they were of 'pure European descent'. Charles A. Cooke, whose father had succeeded General Charles Gordon as chief of the Ever Victorious Army, was not able to do this, for his mother was Chinese. Cooke had left his job in Peking and independently made his way to London with a recommendation for a commission, but was rejected because of his parentage. He was welcome to join the ranks, he was told: no, thank you, Cooke responded, and returned home, furious at meeting such discrimination.[34]

Another twenty-five men joined King Edward's Horse (as would Cooke's brother, in the ranks). The council's Public Works Department crowd joined the Royal Engineers. So did American Sam Glenn, a 'wild' character, reported his former chief, who had deserted from the Customs to sail. (Having quickly reached the front line, he would be discharged in June 1915 on account of his US citizenship). Alexander Scougall rejoined the Royal Marines, but some of those who had intended rejoining old units followed Hilton-Johnson into the Green Howards. Bertie 'Kid' Laurence got a commission in the Westminster Dragoons, as befitted one of Shanghai's 'most prominent jockeys', though joining the cavalry was to prove a frustrating move for men who wanted a quick crack at the enemy. Most of those who signed up for regular army units found themselves move much more swiftly towards the action.

On 16 December Alfred Grimble and some of his pals from the SMP set off to Aylesbury, Buckinghamshire to join the regiment. They dawdled a little, and after their two months confinement in the *Suwa Maru*'s hold, who can blame them? They stopped for the night on the way, and went to a cinema, 'but as strangers we were looked on with suspicion having eventually to explain our-selves to the local Police, we being suspected German spies'. These rowdy Shanghai exotics alarmed the local populace. 'After a lot of explaining and producing our documents,' Grimble remembered, 'we were allowed to go. Really to us, the whole situation was amusing.' They took a car to Aylesbury, reported for duty, were given ten days' leave, came back on 29 December and then 'started soldiering in earnest'. Others arrived at the camp in the meantime: Irish policeman George William Bradish, Shanghai's finest goalkeeper, and Thomas Howarth from Yangtszepoo Station, both appointed company sergeant majors; Detective William Kay, soon made quartermaster sergeant; Frank Reuter, machine gun sergeant; Jack Reynolds, made a transport corporal; and Ernest Fearn, and others. 'So you see Sir,' wrote Grimble to Kenneth McEuen, who had replaced Hilton-Johnson as superintendent of police, 'men from your command soon "made good" and kept up the reputation of the best and of the SMP.'[35]

They were patriots, these men of Shanghai, and they wanted to do their duty and stick it to the enemy. 'I fully considered, being an ex-serviceman, it was up to me to go and do my bit in the common cause', wrote Grimble. But he was a Shanghai patriot too, as many of them were; they kept in touch with the community back in Shanghai. A steady stream of chatty letters arrived on the P&O mail steamers that docked in the Huangpu from the men of the British contingent and their peers – for three other groups had answered the call to arms by the end of 1914, although none as large as the *Suwa Maru* contingent, nor so rapturously cheered on their way. The China Association's London secretary, Harold Wilcox, also sent reports back to Shanghai as he collated news from the men. And the weekly *North China Herald*, occasionally available, allowed some of those overseas to keep up with events in Shanghai, as well as the movements of their fellow Shanghailanders. Kid Laurence read his copies in Egypt, and he passed them on to others. This rich press – which was also uncensored, a source of some consular disquiet – means that one can follow Grimble and his pals in the pages of the *North China Daily News* as they route-marched around the sodden Hertfordshire countryside and up and down the Chiltern hills into the spring of 1915.

They were billeted on local houses (and felt they were fattening their hosts rather than getting the army's money's worth), and found themselves bemused by the local people, and even more so by the Yorkshire min-ers who largely filled the battalion: 'these pitmen are a tough lot, but good'. Kitchener blue-serge uniforms started to be replaced by service khaki from January, but many of the men were still training with dummy wooden rifles. And for three months by then, since leaving Shanghai, they had roughed it – certainly by China coast standards. They were still eager to do their bit, but they certainly missed the sweet comforts of their life back by the Huangpu. Oh, didn't they just; as they picked themselves up from muddy ploughed fields where they had practised night-time bayonet charges, knowing that at the end of the long route-march home they had boots and uniforms to clean, there came to the *Suwa Maru* troopers the eternal lament of the Shanghai exile keening for his servant: 'Oh! for my boy to lend me a hand'.[36]

Extreme Cosmopolites

Sir Everard Duncan Home Fraser, KCMG, son of a British army officer, had arrived in China in 1880, and risen steadily through the ranks of the consular service. Many of his peers affected scholarship of one sort or another, but few were as gifted or as active as Fraser was, and he achieved no little mastery of Chinese. Fraser was also a good administrator, and had steered different British communities through some tricky periods, but nothing except a patient and capacious view of the ingenuities and perversities of human nature could have prepared him for the thorny difficulties of making the war stick in Shanghai.

After all, the China British did not want war, or if they must have it, they did not want it in their backyard. Again and again came variations on the same refrain: the war must be confined, it could not possibly be allowed to dissolve relationships out here; the Shanghai, or

Tianjin, or Hankou Germans or Austrians were a good lot; they were partners, colleagues, friends. 'This war is a terrible business,' wrote Sir Francis Aglen, Peking-based Inspector General of the Chinese Maritime Customs, to his German subordinate A. Heinrich Wilzer, who was commissioner at Qingdao.

> It is a thousand pities it could not be confined to Europe but must invade the Far East where our countries have so many mutual interests and where we English have so many German personal friends.

Japan had declared war on Germany on 23 August, and since then had been preparing its forces to land in Shandong and capture the German leased territory, in which Qingdao was the key prize. Aglen offered to accommodate Wilzer's wife and children when they shipped out of the soon-to-be besieged port to Peking. 'Good luck to you,' he wrote, 'take care of yourself . . . Keep out of the way of shot and shell and endeavour to maintain the neutrality of the Customs.'[37]

That neutrality business enraged Fraser. He thought the Customs had knocked any patriotism out of its men, who had so swallowed its ethos that they were useless to him. The Customs had long borne such criticisms, so it took a cool view of their recrudescence in 1914. 'I think you can safely leave me to my own conscience,' wrote Aglen to a senior British subordinate who had written criticising his stance. 'I do what I think best for the Service and the country for the moment – and my reputation can take care of itself.' (In fact, Aglen had the sanction of Sir John Jordan for his policy, which *sotto voce* was designed to protect 'British preponderance' in the service from the Chinese).[38] After all the Customs was, as even Fraser had to acknowledge, a Chinese government agency.

In Shanghai, however, were men who had no such excuse, who in Fraser's eyes hid behind the cosmopolitan character of the settlement and its international status to shirk their duty. He later poured out his scorn in private letters to Sir Jordan:

> The place is full of greedy rascals, chiefly German and American, with a fair number of British "Merchants" whose loyalty is a very feeble defence against profitable traffic with the enemy and some others who retain the original Shanghailander point of view that resented any interference with their accustomed cosmopolitan dealing.[39]

There were genuine concerns about too rigid an adherence to legislation that forbade trading with the enemy. While it might deny some succour to Germany, it was thought it could actually do more damage to British trade in the short-term (a peculiarity of the structure of British trade with China was that many Manchester-based firms, for example, relied almost exclusively on German agents), and some worried that it would irreparably degrade the British commercial position.

The China British did not on the whole relish upsetting the status quo, which had proved so advantageous, but they really did fear the long-term threat, especially from Britain's East Asian ally, Japan, which by 7 November had broken the German defences at Qingdao and taken its surrender. WE Leveson, the municipal council's secretary, put it bluntly when he came to Fraser and complained about 'hotheads' – Fraser raised an eyebrow at this term – who wanted to 'turn Figge off the Council at the next election'. Leveson praised the German councillor 'extravagantly' and he stated baldly that he 'did not mind taking orders from a German but could not stomach a Jap'.[40] Fraser was caustic about such 'race prejudice', which he thought could only play into German hands, but he did recognise that many worried more pragmatically about Japan's growing strength in China.[41]

Shanghai Britons and their allies did still worry about the Germans, or rather about the new ones flooding into the neutral settlement from hostile cities elsewhere. And Fraser's alleged traitors in the Customs had sons in uniform: Shanghai Customs Commissioner Unwin lost his before the end of the war's first year. But as the council recruited new units into its volunteer corps to counter the perceived Chinese threat, it panicked about the Germans. A new Austrian Company had been formed to help strengthen settlement defences, and even when membership was restricted to permanent residents and excluded the refugees arriving in Shanghai from British Hong Kong or Japan, it meant that the combined German and Austrian volunteer companies numbered 170 men, armed with Lee Enfield's finest rifles, and their 'energetic drilling' frightened people into thinking that local violence was afoot. Fraser knew the company was too few in number to mount any threat, but he remained exasperated that 'of course' the council could do nothing to hamper Britain's enemies, its hands being tied by its international status, and by neutral or hostile consuls zealously alert to British machinations. At least the national companies of the SVC no longer exercised together, and went through their drills and training in different parts of the settlement. It averted some potential bother.

Getting rid of Heinz Figge from the council was one of Fraser's objectives. Early on as things moved to a war footing, he wrote confidently of getting the British electorate to do their duty and having the German replaced at the next election with a Japanese councillor. It would be a practical gesture of respect, a 'just and graceful concession' to the ally that had already demonstrated its commitment to the Allied cause by knocking out Qingdao. British voters by custom ensured the informally agreed balance of nationalities on the council by placing the minority nationals at the top of their ballot paper (they voted for men to fill the full list of seats). But Leveson's view of the Japanese was widely shared, and who in their heart of hearts believed that they had taken Qingdao for any but their own reasons? To complicate matters the Japanese seemed to have shut the port and seized British property there. Fraser was confident that he could 'intimate indirectly' that Figge should be struck out and a Japanese elected instead, but as the election loomed in late January he realised that popular opinion was with Leveson. The Japanese circulated leaflets urging British voters to list Akira Ishii, local manager of the NYK shipping line, but while Figge came bottom of the poll, Ishii failed to get on to the council. On reflection Jordan thought they had pushed the people 'perhaps too far', and 'they have exercised their rights as free voters to reject' the advice.[42] Leveson had caught the mood better than Fraser.

Elsewhere the people exercised their rights, as they saw them, to protect British interests and property. One such was the Shanghai-headquartered Anglo-German Brewery Company, whose prize-winning plant in Qingdao was, after 7 November, in Japanese hands.[43] Empire and beer had advanced into China hand firmly in hand: as foreign armies marched in they called for foreign drink. In 1903 the Anglo-German Brewery

Company had cleared ground in the Qingdao city outskirts with a view to giving it to them. The British and German directors of the firm were ambitious. Their chairman, Alexander McLeod, was based in Shanghai and a pillar of the community: Race Club chairman, St Andrews Society president, and director or chairman of many of the settlement's public companies. He had made his greatest mark on the city by founding the Shanghai Waterworks. One necessity sated, he had turned to another, and to Anglo-German beer. A prospectus was issued and finance raised. A modern electrified factory was constructed at Qingdao – 'the most modern in the East', according to its literature. Ownership of wells to supply the water was secured; a brewmaster was recruited from Germany; the German company Slevogt and Co. was appointed its sole selling agent. Casks and bottles of Gold Export were despatched to Tianjin, Shanghai, Vladivostok and various Siberian ports. Its dark bock beer gained the first big market, as well as a gold medal and diploma at the Munich Beer Festival. So this transnational enterprise shipped beers brewed in a German colony by a British company, incorporated in Hong Kong, headquartered in Shanghai, out to Russia, and to the full range of Chinese treaty ports. It was a classic China coast enterprise.

With the onset of the war, the difficulty for the British directors of the firm and their shareholders was to disentangle themselves from German interests without destroying the company, and so too a British asset. The need to do this was exacerbated by the Japanese military authorities, who threatened to seize the plant, and who were surprised to discover, given its location, name, product, and staff, that it was technically British. Yet the company's shares were sixty per cent German-owned. The German directors were replaced, all the German employees, bar one, were sacked, Slevogt lost the agency to a Chinese firm, and the company was put on a British footing with a new name: Tsingtao Brewery. The one retained employee betrayed the superficiality of these changes: Hermann Henssler, chief brewmaster, without whom there was no beer, and so no business. It also emerged that the German Max Hoerter remained as a non-executive director (and held the greatest number of shares). War is, of course, as much about self-harm as about harming enemy interests: this British company was not deemed British enough, and so had to be shut down. The directors wound it up and sold it to a Japanese brewery.

This was one example among many others, and such disputes and manoeuvres piled up on the consulate desks, greatly adding to the workload of Fraser and his staff in Shanghai, and taxing their patience. These demonstrated the genuine difficulties of splitting apart British and enemy interests, and doing so in a zone where British writ was incomplete, and where such condominium and transnational endeavour had once positively been encouraged. The British directors of Tsingtao – Clarence Ward Wrightson, James Johnston, John Prentice, E. Jenner Hogg, stalwart Shanghailanders all – will hardly have wished to chuck away such a profitable concern. But they and others also genuinely wanted to preserve it as a British company, hoping that Britain would emerge in a stronger, not a weaker, commercial position in China after the war. And everybody liked Max Hoerter, another pillar of the Shanghai community welded into the world of his British counterparts and their businesses. Like them he lived in a large residence – 'The Poplars' – on the leafy Bubbling Well Road, and he was married to Johnston's daughter.

Shanghai cosmopolitanism was a family affair as well as an opportunistic enterprise, always pushing legal boundaries. The directors were all of them honest and honourable men, but they were honest and honourable Shanghai-style. They had between them 185 years experience in working in Shanghai's environment – the oldest among them had come out in 1857, before the International Settlement was established, when the council itself was barely three years old.[44] They were of a Shanghai mind. In Fraser's view, they were all wholly corrupted by cosmopolitan thinking.

Max Hoerter had also been involved in the biggest

local controversy of the war's first six months: should the autumn races be held as usual, and if so, what should be done about the proceeds? Was it right that while men died in France and Belgium their compatriots, indeed their friends, neighbours and family, should be indulging themselves in the community's great pastime? Little discussion was had about continuing the yacht club regattas, the paper hunt, or the rest of the settlement's frantic roster of sporting fixtures, but these involved no betting, and the seeming decadence and insensitivity of holding November's autumn meet was discussed at great length in editorials and on the correspondence pages.

'There is no personal animosity between the people here,' wrote one woman who thought it should go ahead. An objector thought that opportunity had arisen for Shanghai's Britons to 'prove that our patriotism is a quick and living patriotism and not the mere emasculated shadow of that great sentiment'. 'What are you British doing in Shanghai?' another reported being asked, and could say that 'nothing' was the likely answer. Cancel the meeting, some cried. Oh, where will that end? others responded. Even the King is still entering his horses into meetings back home, let us keep our spirits up! Well, wrote 'Griffin' (the local term for a new recruit), 'if life in the Far East where one jostles against strange notions and stranger customs' was going to shape him to 'play skittles while Europe is a charnel house and my brothers are amongst the corpses, then the sooner I quit the model settlement the better for my soul'.[45]

The races went ahead, as the *Suwa Maru* waited in Penang. Hoerter was a long-serving steward, so took part as usual, overseeing the Pari Mutuel – the betting pool. It was a good meet, though the punters missed jockeys Kid Laurence, Arthur Nugent and 'Dolly' Dalgarno, who were kicking their heels in Penang on their way west. Henry Morriss's stable took five cups, his chestnut Chesterfield winning three of them, an altogether great improvement over the spring results. Consciences were cleared when the club donated half the profits to a 'Special Fund for the Relief of Distress Caused by the War', and the great owners made substantial donations too, not least Morriss, who owned the *North China Daily News*, with $500.[46] They refused to curtail future meetings though; they wanted their sport and they wanted it in full. But Max Hoerter stepped back from his stewardship.

So Shanghai raised funds for the war effort as only it could. As well as the race club, the rubber companies – their reputations still tarnished by the bubble of 1910 – made significant contributions. An Overseas Aircraft Fund was also formed, and remitted funds, and Trooper Roach of King Edward's Horse, who had left with the third contingent, wrote excitedly back from France having spotted an aircraft clearly marked 'Shanghai Britons' in honour of the fund (and riddled with bullet holes).[47] Shanghailanders raised money through garden fetes, fancy-dress dances, and concerts. There were the receipts from charity amateur pantomimes, *Ali Baba* and *Cinderella*, and from the 1916 Amateur Billiards Championship. They collected and sent 120 pairs of binoculars home, as well as used (but complete) packs of playing cards. There was a fund for wounded Australians, one to buy tobacco for Irish troops, and another to send furs to Italian soldiers. They danced and performed, and held 'At Homes' to raise money for Belgian and Russian Jewish refugees, rounding up society from the pages of the *Ladies Red Book*. Donations were collected for soldiers' dependants, and for the wounded, and those in captivity, and all was recorded and published as the efforts of the 'Shanghai Britons'. They had always mixed charity with pleasure: before the war they gathered in aid of the Anti-Kidnapping League or the famine districts of China, but now they had reasons for patriotic parties, and a need to demonstrate that they were doing their bit.

Wartime Shanghai had more than a few surreal moments. The manoeuvres of the companies of the SVC had been choreographed carefully to keep the men from the belligerent nations apart, but Colonel RN Bray, who had replaced Bruce as SVC commander, was surely rare among British regular army officers in 1915 in having units of armed Germans and Austrians under his command. Keep your enemies close, the saying goes: fine logic, but liable in practice to be misread. When Bray finally left Shanghai on 23 March 1915 to take up a post at home, the corps paraded along the Bund in his honour, Germans and Austrians alongside their enemies. Such 'good feeling and sportsmanship', it was remarked, 'must have appealed deeply to the Commandant'. Rudolph Buck composed a 'March Colonel Bray' in his honour, a 'very popular item' when it was performed at his farewell dinner.

German musicians remained as vital to Shanghai life as German brewers. In fact, the council had asked the Japanese consul general late in 1914 if it could have its Germans back. Buck's ensemble was considerably weakened by the fact that four men who had rushed to Qingdao to rejoin the colours were now prisoners in Japanese hands (a fifth had been killed in action). The musical life of Shanghai was suffering a decline in quality. No, the consul general replied, very regrettably, the army will not allow their release.[48] So Shanghailanders had to strut their stuff in the SVC, and dance and idle in ballroom or the Public Gardens, to greatly degraded musical accompaniment.

But events off the south-west coast of Ireland now heralded a big shift in public feeling in Shanghai. On 7 May 1915 the sinking by a German submarine of the

Cunard liner RMS *Lusitania*, sailing from New York to Liverpool, electrified opinion internationally. The *Lusitania* was carrying a substantial contraband cargo of munitions, heading for the British war machine, but it was also carrying over 1260 passengers, including over 150 US citizens, as well as its 700 crew. The death toll was 1201, including the majority of the US passengers on board. German officials were quick to point out that the passengers had been publically warned – through their New York newspaper advertisements – that the ship was a target and that it was carrying munitions. In strictly legal terms the *Lusitania* was a legitimate target; but it was a spectacular if not fatal own goal for German attempts to build support overseas.

German army atrocities against civilians and prisoners in the early weeks of the war in Belgium and France had already been seized on by Allied propagandists, and had stoked anti-German sentiment.[49] In the two weeks before the sinking German forces had used poison gas against Allied forces for the first time, and zeppelins had raided English east-coast towns. Now the press could report how the *Lusitania* sank to the sound of shrieking children, and a wave of popular anti-German violence swept parts of Britain.

'THE CRESCENDO OF GERMAN CRUELTY', screamed the *North China Daily News*. Stories spread rapidly of German celebrations, of the Kaiser giving a half-holiday to German schoolchildren 'to commemorate the murder of forty babies under one year of age', as the paper put it. There was no truth to this, but it fuelled Germanophobia. The Germans were even celebrating in Shanghai, it was claimed, holding *Lusitania* parties at the Club Concordia, and festivities at the German school. 'He who not only condones but derives pleasure from the commission of crime is no whit less guilty than the actual perpetrators,' the *Daily News* declared. All talk of 'sportsmanship' was gone. The German consul firmly denied all of these allegations in a note published in the *Municipal Gazette*, and the host of one of the supposed celebrations also wrote to put the record straight, but the challenge was laid down in letters to the press: 'Do Shanghai Germans approve of the *Lusitania* atrocity?' asked DM Gubbay. They were given little space in which to respond, not least because the Shanghai British set about striking a crucial blow against German interests; one that was perhaps most symbolic of their often parochial view of the war, which they would fight on their own terms, at least in the International Settlement.[50]

The *Lusitania* news broke on the last day of the race club's spring meeting. Attendance had been larger than usual over the week, the scene 'gay and animated'. 'Pretty dresses there always are and this year they were smarter even than usual,' reported the *North China Herald*. Rudolph Buck's diminished band played a refreshing blend of 'popular music' and 'old airs'. Henry Morriss's stable excelled itself (seven winners this time). But then the stewards instructed the secretary to ask all forty German members 'not to make use of the Grand Stand, premises or compound of the Club until further notice'.[51] Here was real action at last. 'Feeling here against the Germans is running very high', reported Customs Statistical Secretary FE Taylor, 'and they are being elbowed out of all clubs.'

And so they were. Their presence at the Shanghai Club was deemed 'objectionable', and the nineteen German members were asked to 'refrain from entering'. (In the immediate aftermath of the sinking it could be more violent: German businessman Theodore Meyer, long-term resident in the settlement, was physically thrown out of the race club by one of its British members. A matter for the stewards, a passing British policeman told him, not for the law.[52]) Similar notes went out from the country club, rowing club and *Cercle sportif français*. Taylor thought it tiresome that it taken so long for such action to take place, not least as he felt it had so weak a cause (the Germans, 'after giving fair warning, succeed in sinking a steamer full of ammunition and supplies for their enemy', he wrote). Still, the Germans were 'the ancient Goths disguised in a thin veneer of civilization which in time of peace more or less covers up their innate barbarism'.[53] Indignant at their treatment, the Germans and Austrians in the rowing club declared that they considered themselves expelled, and were 'barbaric' enough to threaten to melt down the cups they held unless their membership subscriptions for the year were returned to them. 'Sport,' announced one correspondence, 'does not make gentlemen of them.'[54]

In their own clumsy way, over matters trivial and important, the Shanghai British were falling into line with their compatriots elsewhere. The *Lusitania's* sinking fired them up, despite the continuing sense of ambivalence. News had also arrived reporting the first death in action of one of the Shanghai volunteers, Albert Radcliffe, ex-Customs, born in China, one of thirty who had sailed on 30 October the previous year on the *Atsuta Maru*.[55] On 24 May 1915, with this news fresh to hand and their clubs now free of the enemy, and on a day of 'perfect weather', the British celebrated the first Empire Day of the war. This patriotic event was still a relatively new addition to the British calendar, and largely aimed at children, but everyone took it to heart. Allied flags flew high and proud; boy scouts marched to the consulate and raised the Union Flag in its grounds. Consul General Fraser agreed to the 'spontaneous request' of the British members of the SVC to inspect the company. The Bund was crowded by late morning as the Sikh police of the SMP and the volunteers formed up and marched along it and into the consulate grounds. There, at noon, Fraser received their salute and congratulated them on a 'magnificent display of loyalty and patriotism which I shall have the greatest pleasure in reporting to my superiors'. The national anthem was sung, three cheers hurrahed, echoing out and down the Bund, and penetrating even the closed windows of the Concordia Club, past which many of those present then marched proudly on their way to a few cool drinks at the Shanghai Club's long bar.

That night, as British and French tram-company vehicles traversed the city all lit up with red, white and blue lights, and the words '*Honneur et Patrie*', or 'God Save the King', the Overseas Club organised a 'National Concert' that played to a packed house at the Lyceum Theatre. Shanghai celebrated the contribution of the Dominions to the war and, implicitly, its own readiness to fight and its patriotism, while the ladies sold sweet peas to raise money for the *Lusitania* fund. Fraser did report all this to his superior in Peking, and stressed that it was a 'spontaneous' display. This day of flag-waving, martial spirit and song meant Britons began to shed the taint of cosmopolitanism that still seemed to infuse their every encounter; it marked a move to conform with the total war footing of the British state.[56] Ambivalence remained, but not perhaps on 4 August, the first anniversary of the war, when volunteers, police and scouts attended a packed service at Holy Trinity Cathedral. All the Allied consuls attended, presided over by the senior – longest-serving – consul, Belgian Daniel Siffert, who had escaped German-occupied Brussels early in the war, returning to Shanghai in January 1915 to a rapturous welcome on the Bund from a crowd of several hundred. After the service the SVC Britons marched out and along the Nanjing Road, past the Concordia to the Bund. On the foreshore opposite Jardine, Matheson & Co., standing next to the *Iltis* monument, they drew up and were dismissed. That evening hundreds of people gathered on the race club grandstand to hear speeches from their consuls supporting a motion to do all that they could to drive a victory home.[57]

As 1915 continued they marched the streets and shouted loud, draping the buildings of the settlement with their national flags when they could. They did not possess the settlement, and their enemies could march within it also, but whenever possible Britons took temporary charge of the Nanjing Road, Bubbling Well and the Bund by parading through them, and as often as not made sure to pass the Club Concordia, taunting its members with cheers and their uniformed massed ranks. Young Britons took their voices into Shanghai's nightlife too: 'a gang of stupid youths howl "Rule Britannia" and other patriotic songs', complained one Danish observer in a letter to the *North China Daily News*. Good clean fun, enjoyed by all, replied one of them, shortly off to 'do my "little bit"', and it was he felt a 'rather refreshing' sign of 'enthusiasm' among Shanghai's Britons. Plenty of Germans were also heading off to do their bit, though facing greater difficulties in getting back to Europe. They went via the United States on neutral steamship lines, and without fanfares on the Bund.[58]

The Shanghai British shouted loud, and they got stuck in. By mid-January it had been estimated that over 200 men had sailed home to join up in the five contingents organised by the China Association. Some policemen disappointed at not being selected for the *Suwa Maru* had attempted to engineer their own dismissals through insubordination, so that they could get away with these later groups.[59] Many other residents had made their own way to Britain. Meanwhile Annie de Sausmarez, wife of the British Supreme Court judge, had outlined on 25 September 1914 a plan for a scheme to supply garments and bandages for British troops. A British Women's Work Association was established and rapidly got to work, sending its first packages to the Queen Mary's Needlework Guild in November, and relaying thereafter a steady supply home. The Shanghai British, as they got on with their business, certainly believed that none now could impugn their patriotism.[60] Sir Everard Fraser still had much cause for concern, but his early difficulties in getting his charges motivated were now starting to be overcome.

Hill 70

In Hertfordshire, Quartermaster Sergeant William Kay had been so eager to get to the war that he deserted his regiment to join another unit as a private in late May 1915. The Shanghai policeman felt he'd have a quicker chance of seeing some action if he quit a post where he did nothing but dole out supplies. The Gordon Highlanders took him on, for when he filled in the forms it seems that he was a little imprecise about his prior military career. Eventually the Military Police traced Kay during his embarkation leave. The mine labourer's son from Falkirk had joined the SMP in 1907 after six years in the Scots Guards, and was one of the older men who had sailed from China. Shanghai looked after its own, and at his court martial in late June it was his fellow *Suwa Maru* recruit, Captain John Douglas, barrister, who successfully defended him, defeated the charge, and helped Kay back into the army's good graces: Kay rejoined the 10th Battalion of the Yorkshire Regiment, happily enough for him as a private. Douglas and Kay had been in court actions together before, back in Shanghai, but then the Scot was giving evidence against the lawyer's clients, not appearing in the dock as one of them.[61]

Kay had reason enough to be impatient as the spring wore on. After the dash from Shanghai the men of the Yorkshire Regiment found themselves marching about the Chilterns shouldering dummy rifles for month after endless damp month. Lacking weapons, equipment and uniforms, their training was little advanced by April, not least because while the men of Shanghai were proud to watch John Douglas 'strutting about in his Captain's uniform', Douglas and his fellow officers simply lacked the experience to train the men under their command.[62] It was only in mid-May 1915 that the men had been moved out of private billets into a proper camp.

Douglas, a naval admiral's son, had rushed to Qingdao from Shanghai to get some experience as the siege there had begun, for poor eyesight initially prevented him securing an easy commission, but behind-the-lines observation was no substitute for the mature professionalism of the regular army. The regiment's colonel, Arthur De Salis Hadow, had come back from five years of retirement, but had barely seen action at all in his thirty-two years in the army. Major Wilfrid Dent, second in command, a martinet who had not been too popular initially (even Hadow thought him fussy), had been out of the army for longer, but had seen combat relatively recently, for he had taken part in the suppression of the Boxer uprising back in 1900 with Hilton-Johnson and the Weihaiwei Regiment.

By early summer they had weapons – Japanese rifles in fact, reported Shanghai-born Tom Wade, who had joined the contingent from a job with British American Tobacco. The former Shanghai walking champion, whose 'defective vision' had initially seen him rejected for service, Wade really was a true Shanghailander, born and bred; his father was originally born there too, in 1846, one of the very first British Shanghai babies. In June and July Wade sent updates on the evolving preparations of the 10th Yorkshires. They were now training as a division – the 21st – 20 000 men marching together through Aylesbury (it took them eight hours), and 'all as keen as mustard to get to the front'. The men moved to Aldershot, Hampshire in the early summer, marching in easy stages, and at one point were reviewed by the King and Lord Kitchener, Minister for War, who 'both gave us a good word', reported council Public Works Department Inspector Frederick Turner. 'Very fine,' said Kitchener.[63] He might have done better to give the men good socks instead, or any socks in fact: for months none had been supplied to the battalion, and the men had trained wearing cloth foot-bandages instead.

Many of the former soldiers who came back by the

Suwa Maru rapidly found themselves promoted corporals and sergeants to train their novice colleagues, such was the acute shortage of experienced men at all levels across Kitchener's 'New Army' of hurriedly recruited British civilians. Tom Wade took delivery of his metal identification disk, final pieces of kit, and sat through lectures about poison gas, but instead of getting to the action, found himself compiling returns as an orderly clerk. Frederick Turner was training signallers. His three brothers were already in France, he reported, and the youngest 'still quite cheerful'. The men of the 10th Yorkshires were itching to join them. Hilton-Johnson left the regiment in June for divisional headquarters, but as the senior officers were shuffled around, the 10th Yorks was joined by yet another former Shanghai man, Charles MacLellan, who had spent some years in the port before moving to British Malaya in 1912, and was known to some from his six years in the SVC. The battalion's Shanghai contingent was getting even more numerous.

Frustration in Aylesbury and Aldershot was no doubt exacerbated by the news from those peers who had gone into regular army units, although there was pause for thought there. Scotsman Alexander Scougall was one of the oldest of the *Suwa Maru* men, having served twenty-two years in the Royal Marine Light Infantry, latterly in China, before joining the SMC Public Works Department in 1912. Within two months of arriving in London and signing back on in Chatham he was on his way to the front, and Scougall took part in the main landings at Gallipoli on 25 April 1915. This attempt to force the Straits was to be one of the greatest Allied defeats of the war. The landings were stoutly opposed by Ottoman troops, and the terrain was impossible.

Scougall was part of an attack launched on 3 May up a ravine against enemy positions. In the early-morning light, machine gun and rifle fire rained down on the men. Snipers killed many of those who survived, including Scougall, shot through the eye a few hours into the fighting. 'Poor old "Jock"', wrote a comrade, 'a good soldier and a staunch one.' He was laid in 'a little trench with others', high up a steep cliff, and given a Christian burial, it was stressed. But they were all given proper burials, at least in letters home: the fact that hundreds, thousands of men, were left where they fell was often too ghastly to report. Jockey Bertie Laurence also got to the Dardanelles later that summer. Dispirited beyond measure by the death of his brother in France in August, however, Laurence reportedly half-willed the killing that came to him at twilight in no-man's-land on 9 September. 'I shall be grateful when this is all over,' wrote one correspondent of the campaign, 'for it is worse than murder.'[64]

In Aldershot things finally seemed to be moving, so much so that one of the contingent belatedly got cold feet and promptly deserted.[65] In late July both Hilton-Johnson and the commander Colonel Hadow had gone to France, and 'the dawn of the day of promise' seemed to be 'fast approaching'. After an intensive month of musketry training in August (Arthur Castle from the SMC Public Health Department and Fred Turner coming top in their company), the men of Shanghai marched out of Whitley Camp near Godalming at six p.m. on 9 September, reached Folkestone by just before midnight, and disembarked after a smooth passage from a small steamer at Boulogne at a quarter past three the following morning.[66] 'All very glad to get away. Worked to death, up all night before leaving,' wrote Major Dent to a friend in Shanghai. They were, remembered Alfred Grimble, 'looking forward to doing our bit'. They felt more than ready. But the official history of the war, published in 1928, exercised a note of carefully phrased retrospective caution: 'In general', concluded its author, Sir James Edmonds, the 21st Division, along with the 24th, now also deploying across to France, was 'thought to be better trained than they really were'.[67] The New Army divisions were about to head into a battle the like of which the British army had never before seen, and into a controversy that still echoes down the years. The Shanghai British were there in the heart of it, right in the middle of the Battle of Loos.

First there was another train to Watten, France, and

nine days in billets at the small village of Houlle. From there Arthur Castle wrote east again on 20 September, pleased to be over the channel at last, and close to being able to 'try and even matters up a little on the right side', by which he meant for those with right on their side. Persistent stories about German 'devilish methods of warfare', and news of zeppelin raids on England and of the use of poison gas and flame-throwers had fired up the men. Germany 'deserved all that is coming to her'. Castle's billet, a barn, was well below the Shanghai norm, and aside from some of the 10th Yorkshires, was inhabited by a wide range of mammals and 'smaller fry'. His colleagues back in the Health Department would go 'balmy' [sic], he wrote: it was worse than even some of the Chinese houses they had to inspect. The 'stench beats China', wrote one of his Shanghai colleagues from another section of the line, praise indeed. The men were at least well equipped now with socks, 300 pairs of which had just been received by the regiment, for the Women's Work Association back in Shanghai now had a volunteer department that targeted some of its supplies to men who had joined in the Shanghai contingents.

On the 20 September, the battalion began a wearying series of three-night marches that took them closer and closer to the front line in the Pas-de-Calais, east of Béthune, where on the morning of 21 September 950 guns had began an incessant bombardment of the

German defences, aiming to destroy the wire and the infrastructure of defence behind the main enemy lines. The weather turned foul. At the small village of Burbure the battalion spent the nights of 22 and 23 September, then marched out on the night of the 24th, bivouacked in a field and slept if possible as the rain came down and the guns fired on. Before they marched Colonel Hadow had given them a 'fiery oration which moved the men a great deal', Tom Wade reported. Such gingering up was going on across the front as 75 000 British troops, and further south many more French soldiers, prepared for action.

On the morning of the 25th the guns upped their tempo and at five-fifty a.m., thousands of newly installed cylinders started to release chlorine gas into no-man's-land. It was the first time the British had used the weapon, and it was critical to the British 1st Army Commander, General Sir Douglas Haig's plans for the day. The wind would steadily take the gas across the German lines, leaving death and panic in its wake. It seemed simple, and where conditions allowed, 'a dense cloud, thirty to fifty feet high' formed along the battle front, but it failed to drift consistently over the German trenches, for the wind proved slight. Moreover the British lines meandered, and the gas did too, back into their positions and over the waiting attackers.

Forty minutes after the gas was released, six divisions of the British 1st Army, wearing gas masks through which they could hardly see, attacked along a wide front, north and south of the village of Loos. This was the largest assault yet made in British military history. In the southern sector Scottish units and the London Regiment smashed spectacularly two miles into German-held territory across five miles of the front, taking Loos itself. Haig's plan worked perfectly there, but overall it was as black a day as any that could be imagined. The 'big push' was ill conceived, ill planned, and ill organised. It had also been hurriedly elaborated at French insistence. The actual objectives were vague, the terrain treacherous, the weather rotten. Tactics were inconsistent, and sometimes already known to be inadequate. There were not enough guns, shells or grenades. Roads behind the lines were badly managed, and hideously congested. There was poor communication between infantry and artillery; between units in the field and their headquarters; and between the officer commanding, General Haig, and the British Commander in Chief Sir John French. There were at least enough men (though not in the right places at the right time), and they fought bravely, but as Sir James Edmonds later noted of the engagement: 'Bravery is not sufficient to win battles.'[68] And the heavily outnumbered Germans also fought like tigers, their machine guns inflicted numbing levels of casualties on the attackers.

As the day wore on the 10th Yorkshires moved from

their reserve position to join the assault, as the two New Army divisions were thrown into the battle. The men found themselves moving towards battered Loos village at a quarter past three in the afternoon, past the devastation, hundreds of British dead alone, mostly Scottish troops, casualties of the initial assault, which had been loudly broadcast by the gas that now lingered on in low-lying land and caused eyes to smart. And then the men of Shanghai and the pitmen they had trained with went forward to attack. They had been in France for just two weeks, and they had never been in the frontline, or even seen it. They had marched for three hours, past 'fellows struggling along' in the opposite direction, 'some with their heads, arms, legs covered with blood and bandages, and some with no bandages on at all, but just nursing their hurts'. John Douglas saw 'horrible sights', and now shells started to fall amongst them. Still in full marching order, packs on their backs, overcoats on, they had been rushed forward, formed up in open order, in columns of platoons and moved forward.

Their target was Hill 70, just east of the village of Loos. So rapidly had they come forward, however, that they had no detailed map of the area, and only a vague idea of where or what Hill 70 was. The brigade commander at least knew, but his orders to his divisional commanders were vague: get there, find out what has happened, hold it or take it, whichever is necessary.

It was the story of the day across the British lines. So they marched four abreast, platoons a hundred yards apart, down the old road and across the British and captured German trenches, which proved slow going, for there had not been much time to bridge these. Major Dent calmed John Douglas's nerves by chatting about Shanghai as they rode alongside the men, showing him photographs of the Bund that he had brought along. German gunners spotted the column and opened fire, destroying its transport. The battalion now moved across country to take up positions near Loos cemetery, but moved in the wrong direction, crossed the British line and attacked, walking into a hail of machine-gun and sniper fire. From the reports they had received, their officers had thought that they should have an 'easy task' of it. Here, among 'men dropping fairly frequently', at what they wrongly thought was the bottom of the hill, Arthur Castle passed policeman George Bradish, who had taken a bullet through the leg. As Castle moved by, a young signaller, who was helping Bradish staunch the wound, was shot dead.

Checked by the German defence, the battalion retired and took up a position to extend a hurriedly improvised new British line while half the men were set to clearing Loos village of remaining Germans. Their letters make it clear that like many that day they did not take prisoners. Night fell, and most of the men, who had by now thrown away their coats and packs, spent it in the open, in extended formation, wet through, shivering, hungry and thirsty.

Tom Wade spent the evening retrieving their wounded sergeant major from where he lay in a field, and carrying him three miles back to a dressing station. Joining some bombers on returning to the frontline he ran into a 'heavy cross fire of shrapnel', which took him out of the day's action, but from which, all in all, he had 'a wonderful escape'. The officers – 'a dirty looking lot – everyone was covered in mud from head to foot, wet through, cold and shivering' – sheltered in a captured gun emplacement. Vaughan Craddock got some water boiling in a German mess tin over a fire made from the wicker chests the German shells were transported in. Colonel Hadow produced some powdered carrot soup, and he and Major Dent warmed themselves with this, saving some for their juniors, as bullets and shells 'were whistling about and bits of houses' fell about the place. The men in the fields had no food except their iron rations, preserved meat and biscuits, but eating these simply increased thirsts that could not be quenched, for they had no water either.

As Craddock watched in the early pre-dawn light, the colonel set about writing a letter to his wife, as he had done every day since they arrived in France. 'My darling Maud,' he wrote, 'I wonder if I shall ever finish this or whether this morning is my last on earth.'

> We have had a very terrible time during the last
> 24 hours & in half an hour have to make another
> attack with what I've got of my Battn left with me
> only just over 400.

Hadow had lost his eldest son in mid-June, killed by shellfire at just twenty years old after being gazetted into another battalion of the Yorkshire regiment straight from Sandhurst. The colonel took solace from a deep religious faith, and his knowledge that he was doing his duty 'as I ought to do'. But he was still distraught at the loss, and as bewildered as a man could be by the violence of the day just past, the hours of marching, the hurried leap into action, twelve hours of attack and counter-attack. He and Dent had had a hard job keeping the men together. Many were dead or wounded, others now scattered around Loos. Hadow had confided in his diary from the outset his belief that this 'very big push' would 'entail terrible casualties'. Orders now came to move up and into the new attack, so he signed off quickly: 'I've been saved so far, but it seemed a marvel how I did & now we've to go through it again. The German infantry is no good its their Artillery, Machine Guns & Snipers. We are just off. Good bye with love'.[69]

At nine on the morning of the 26 September, after an hour's bombardment, the British resumed the attack on Hill 70, the first waves partly gaining it, but being badly mauled by continuing German fire. Then it was the turn of the 10th Yorkshires. 'It's got to be done, gentlemen, and after all, we've only got one life to live,' Major Dent had told his officers. Arthur Hadow did his duty, climbed up to the trench parapet to encourage them forward with a shout of 'Charge' and was shot dead, taking a bullet through the neck. Dent followed: 'Now my lads, I want you to follow me and take that trench over there,' he called. Up he got, a singular sight, tall and thin, waving his ash cane in the air. He made it ten yards then fell, dying with a bullet in his side. Policeman Frank Reuter was closest to him, in charge of the machine guns, which, at least, did 'some grand work' that day, before he was wounded in the arm. Arthur Castle was also close by as Geoffrey Turner, an eleven-year veteran of the SVC, now a captain, climbed onto the parapet to urge the dispirited and exhausted men forward. Turner was immediately hit in the leg and threw himself back into the trench. 'Rather hard luck being hit so soon,' he later wrote. Leaving him in the care of another wounded man, Castle went forward, crawling like the others on hands and knees through the long grass until, thirty yards from the German trench, he too was hit. He dragged himself back, living 'a long time in those minutes' as he wriggled away from the wire defending the enemy position.

By this point the battalion had lost its first, second and third in command. And yet they continued to advance, 'in a perfect shower of high explosives, shrapnel and bullets', and a 'Scotch mist of gas'. Charles MacLellan had taken over Turner's company, and the latter, while dressing his leg wound, saw MacLellan 'going up the hill waving his hunting crop and yelling'. 'I can just imagine what he was saying,' Turner continued, for 'his vocabulary was glorious.' Unbelievably, the regiment took the hill. 'The Bosches could not stand our bayonets,' recalled Grimble, 'and it was Mercy Camerade etc but I don't know that they got much.' Vaughan Craddock waved to fellow Jardine man William Cornaby when he saw him, wounded hand roughly bandaged, heading back from the crest that afternoon. 'I can't tell you what happened really,' Craddock wrote, 'as one lost account of all time and things. One saw some horrid sights, but they did not affect me, as one had other things to think of and no time to dwell on the awfulness of it all.' In the face of the withering fire from the regiment's flanks, and bombing from German troops still entrenched in parts of the defences, the men could not hold the hill, and retired exhausted and broken back through the shambles and through Loos, despite efforts to rally them.

'I was one of the lucky ones. Not a scratch,' reported Grimble, but most had not been so lucky. William Kay, who had at last got some action, had been wounded too. Australian Percy Pickburn had been hit by an entrenching tool during some hand-to-hand fighting. But aside from Major Dent, the men of Shanghai had all survived, and although the operation had been a failure, and the Battle of Loos was a signal defeat for the British, they had done what they set out to do when they signed up for the *Suwa Maru* back in October 1914. 'I assure you,' wrote Grimble with some satisfaction, 'that I put one or two in for Shanghai.'[70] Also lost to the war effort that day was Grimble's former chief CD Bruce: one of many British senior officers who had gone too far forward, he was captured by counter-attacking German troops, and would spend the next thirty months in captivity.

The two New Army divisions were widely criticised in the aftermath of the battle, not least by Sir John French, the British commander in chief, seeking a scapegoat for his own failings. Reports of them rambling back like a 'bank holiday crowd', all discipline and spirit broken, have been fixed in understandings of the day by poet and soldier Robert Graves, who watched them retreat. A fairer comment came from closer to home. 'Can you picture their plight?' wrote Hilton-Johnson in a letter published in the *North China Herald*:

> New soldiers, unblooded, thrust into a tearing battle on their first introduction to the real thing; black night, rain, wet through, done to a turn with long marches, no hot food, a murderous machine-gun fire, gas-shells bursting all around, strange country and amateur officers for the most

part – and then can you wonder that things hung fire a bit? In my mind it was the highest trial that new soldiers could have.[71]

Think of all those sweltering days on the *Suwa Maru*, as Hilton-Johnson must have, the training in semaphore, body-building and squad discipline, his lectures on types of conflict irrelevant to the world of gas, shrapnel, machine guns, barbed wire and trenches into which the police chief's former charges were thrown. 'It is marvellous any of us are alive,' Frank Reuter wrote. Hilton-Johnson, the strain already showing in his letter, soon thereafter suffered a nervous breakdown, and was invalided back to Britain and out of the army for good.

French had ordered the reserves to be sent in too late (they were anyway positioned too far back) and was slow even to convey the order, and so the men went in against strengthened defences. The number of British guns and the ammunition available had also been insufficient. And while the men were trained as soldiers and did not want for courage, their officers lacked training and experience. Controversy over the failure, and the root causes of it, led to French's resignation as British commander in chief, but that did not help the men of the *Suwa Maru*.

Telegrams had rattled in swiftly to Shanghai communicating the news of the offensive. 'Glorious charge of the British,' claimed the Reuters correspondent. 'They were irresistible.' They carried trench after trench, and 'the

German dead were piled four deep in some trenches'. But it was a photograph that circulated in the highest reaches of the British government of dead Highland infantry, piled up in front of the single German machine gun that had killed them, that better symbolised the British failure at Loos.[72] German military reports wrote of a 'corpse-field', not a battlefield. At least 22 494 men lost their lives or were missing presumed dead, about 300 of them in the 10th Yorkshires. Thousands more were wounded.[73]

For all that, at Hill 70 on 25–26 September, Shanghai Britons went into action together and fought for the first time. It was probably the largest number of them concentrated in a single unit during the war, fighting together in one battle. Blood stained the snapshots of Shanghai in Wilfrid Dent's pocket as he lay by the parapet at the base of Hill 70 and as Frank Reuter retrieved his personal possessions to send on to his family. There was no trace of cosmopolitanism or ambivalence in the letters home of the 10th Battalion of the Yorkshire Regiment, reproduced in the *North China Daily News*. They hated the Germans: they were Bosches, Huns. They were animals, who 'deserve to be exterminated'. The men reported killing Germans, especially snipers, who were trying to surrender, but who had been firing on them up to the last possible moment. 'That type of animal does not deserve any mercy,' wrote one former SVC machine gunner, now plying the same trade in support of the first day's assault. 'One young chap' who had taken a prisoner, reported Tom Wade, 'took out a photograph of his brother who was killed a little while back, showed it to the German, then killed him.'

Tom Wade was writing back as his comrades lay shivering overnight in the field south-east of Loos, and over the next couple of months one can trace Wade, Reuter, Castle and others as they were moved back to hospitals and convalescent homes in Britain. By the end of 26 September the 10th Yorkshires had moved out of the immediate arena of battle, and for the next three weeks they were mostly in billets at Strazeele, further north, waiting for replacement kit and taking in new drafts of men and officers, including Herbert Such and T. Rowley Evans from the *Suwa Maru*. The latter had been kicking his heels at base censoring letters, and felt he would regret that he had missed the 'big charge' 'to the end of my days'. In mid-October the battalion moved closer to the frontline, and started rotating in and out of the trenches 'to be instructed in trench warfare and duties' – at last, we might think – which took its toll in dead and wounded. After ten days of this the men formally took over a section of the line near Armentières. The weather continued wet, collapsing the sides of the 'rotten' trench or flooding it, and they were constantly at work on repairs. After a break they were back in on the evening of 6 November and the next morning, nosing around no-man's-land in the fog to get a sense of the lie of the terrain. Rowley Evans was spotted and got 'pipped' on the top of his head by a German bullet. He was able to crawl away and back to the British lines, and wrote his account of his lucky escape to Shanghai from hospital in London. Steel helmets were not yet in use in the British Expeditionary Force.[74]

In mid-December Shanghai's British contingent suffered three casualties when the battalion had just come back into the frontline from Armentières. A raid on the German lines from the units to their south brought down some days of heavy bombardment and sniping, and on the 19th a raid by five aircraft equipped with torpedoes. 'And not one of ours could be seen,' wrote the battalion war diarist, while 'the retaliation of our own artillery was very poor'. Tom Wade was one of five men wounded by the sniping, taking a bullet in the chest on 17 December that narrowly missed his heart and lungs and knocked him out of the war for six months. The air raid left craters twelve feet deep and up to thirty-five feet across. As the torpedoes landed in the midst of a two-hour bombardment, Alfred Grimble and another sergeant did what they could to rally the panicked men, keeping them in order for fear that the bombing would be followed by a German assault. Both men were awarded the Distinguished Conduct Medal, but

Grimble took wounds in both legs, as one of the missiles landed barely fifteen feet away, leaving him stunned and part-buried. On 28 December at the Red Cross hospital at Le Touquet both of his legs had to be amputated.[75]

The day before the air raid had been quieter. But while John Douglas was checking the wire early that morning he was hit in the throat by a stray bullet. It was not his first foray into no-man's-land. 'I have only recently learned what weather means in war,' he had written, and reported himself wearing 'sea boots that came up to the thighs, a short oil-skin and a s'ou-wester', scouting the terrain in early-morning mists trying to devise ways to drain the crumbling trenches they were holding. Douglas was still conscious when he was brought back to the British line, and as he was carried into an ambulance that took him to a field hospital. But he died at noon the same day.

A telegram arrived in Shanghai with the news of Douglas's death on 29 December. Just four days earlier the *North China Daily News* had printed a long, chatty letter from the barrister bringing the settlement up to date with the activities of the 10th Yorkshires. He grumbled about army bureaucracy, about having to account from his rotten trench to comfortably billeted staff officers demanding he acknowledge receipt of supplies of jam. Douglas had been spared at Loos: his company commander had been killed and he had taken over 'A'

Company, but he had been ordered to take most of the men and hold a line of captured trenches, and so missed the assault on Hill 70. 'I was lucky,' he wrote 'for, though I had many close calls, I was never touched.' Over thirty per cent of the division could not say the same, but now luck had started to run out for some of the *Suwa Maru* men in the Green Howards.[76]

The death of John Douglas was not the first high-profile death in Shanghai. He was not even the first casualty among its small cadre of barristers. Lieutenant Henry Oppe, who had been one of the organisers of the China Association committee in October 1914, had been killed in Gallipoli in November 1915. Australian-born Captain Loftus Jones had been in France for only a short while before his death in early August of the same year. These three were men at the heart of local society. Jones had been chairman of the Shanghai Club's committee; the trio were fixtures of the paper hunt, the race and rowing clubs, and the SVC; some of them were active freemasons. They had been involved in all the peregrinations of Shanghai's business life, not least the rubber boom, and their loss struck deeper than would the losses of the rankers from Shanghai's British drafts. News back in June of the death of a well-known Shanghai-born Jardine employee, Jack Davidson, who had been on leave when war broke out and had promptly joined the London Scottish, arriving in France while the

Suwa Maru was still a month from England, had added to the sense of a community starting to share in full the burden of British Empire's grief.

On Thursday 30 December Police Court Magistrate GW King delayed the morning's proceedings in Shanghai to pay tribute to his personal and professional friendship with John Douglas, a man from a 'fighting race', of an 'impulsive nature', who 'died as he had lived – an English gentleman'. Early in January Supreme Court Judge Sir Havilland de Sausmarez led a gathering of the Shanghai Bar in the courtroom, in which those present echoed King's language and sentiments. Douglas's was a 'glorious death in the cause of righteousness and of the King and his empire'. Flags at Shanghai's clubs flew at half-mast when the news of his death reached the settlement, as they had for Wilfrid Dent, and as they would several times more. The 'Roll of Honour' began to lengthen. In the aftermath of the conflict each of the clubs, as well as the council and many of the city's businesses, would install their own memorials to their dead colleagues, inscribing their names into Shanghai's buildings.

Perhaps elite Shanghai was better remembered in those ways than the Shanghai constables and sergeants who also dashed home to the war: for in death the community's social cleavages became starker yet. Tributes paid, the Britons living by the Huangpu got on with the business of court or racing, or arranging bazaars and pantomimes to raise money to send tobacco to Tommies, while the British women of Shanghai kept up knitting socks and rolling bandages. Better business as usual than dwelling on the bleak news from France or the Dardanelles: for no quick entry to Berlin was in the offing.

Back to
Business as Usual

Shanghai rushed to war in 1914, and was blooded relatively early in the conflict that consumed so many millions. Ambivalent at first, many of them, and resistant to the inconveniences of total war, which threatened local ruin, the Shanghai British were forced to acknowledge the need to comply by officials, 'monomaniac' and otherwise, who wielded the new instruments of wartime legislation, and who harangued them about their duty to King, Empire and the cause of right. Many were ready to fight, and the sinking of the *Lusitania* led many to hate, but significant numbers still found it hard to reconcile the war's black and white world with their own, for its shades of grey and its ambiguities were the basis on which their Shanghai thrived. And for three years Shanghai remained a strange in-between city, with Germans and Austrians, Britons, Belgians and the French all still sharing the settlement, with China's neutrality in the background, until the Allies nudged the Chinese republic towards declaring for them. Diplomatic relations with Germany were broken off in March 1917, and China declared war on the country on 14 August that year.

For all that Shanghai had its awkward start to the war, it was always part of a wider global community of sentiment, of a British world of language, thought and culture; one that traversed the formal borders of empire and followed men and women whose origins and hearts lay back in the islands that they had left behind, sometimes just months earlier, sometimes generations back. Historians have debated the costs and benefits to Britain of its empire, and in economic terms the results seem inconclusive overall. But in terms of the benefits in 1914, in the example of the men of the *Suwa Maru*, we can see the otherwise invisible returns to the British Isles of the great expansion of the Victorian era. Back they rushed from Shanghai, boxing and drilling as they sailed, and into the war they passed.

They went, each alone with their thoughts into battle, but many were conscious of themselves as men of Shanghai, flying its flag at Hill 70 and elsewhere. Knitting this British Shanghai together was a criss-crossing network of letters, chance and engineered encounters between the men in Flanders or in English hospitals, and at the heart of it all the press, specifically the *North China Daily News* and its weekly mail edition, the *North China Herald*. Its over two and a half thousand subscribers engaged with the paper through its formal correspondence pages, but spoke to each other in various ways through its columns, not least passing on letters received from the front, and sharing news received in other ways.[77]

Even as the men of the *Suwa Maru* were dispersed further and further into the maw of the global British war machine, their identity as the 'Shanghai contingent' stuck fast in the press, in the imaginations of its readers, and among themselves. Standard Oil employee and Boy's Brigade 'veteran' Arthur Brown's army medal card even lists '1st Shanghai Contingent' as his initial unit. Various editions of a Shanghai war book started to be published from December 1915, listing those who were under arms and their fates, and recording the activities of the British Women's Work Association. Shanghailanders could now point to these texts and proclaim themselves true patriots, free of any cosmopolitan taint. By the book's third edition (as *The China War Book*), it listed 1 894 French, British, Belgian and Italian men on active service with the Allied forces, 212 of whom had died. Harold Wilcox at the China Association in London was trying to keep up with 1 500 Britons alone from across China by November 1918. Almost 200 China British men would die in service – and one woman. Dorothy

May Jones was the stepdaughter of a recent acting Customs commissioner at Shanghai. A volunteer nurse, she had drowned when the RMS *Leinster* was torpedoed in the Irish Sea a month before the war's end.[78]

The Shanghai British had, it is true, their odd collective view of the world and of their place within it. This sophisticated urban society seemed together to believe that it lived on a hard-riding frontier. But the riding that was the focus of anxiety and complaint in the summer of 1914 was joy-riding in cars; headlights and horns, not furious driving of horse or carriage. Still, 'men who can ride and shoot' were wanted; men on the *Polynesien* expected to find posts that would use precisely those talents, and many on the *Suwa Maru* joined King Edwards' Horse. But 'cavalry are useless in the Dardanelles,' Kid Laurence had noted, 'so we have to bear our souls in patience here.' John Douglas left his two ponies behind in Shanghai, and died while still puzzling out how to drain a trench. An ability to wield a spade or throw a bomb, not hold a horse's reins, was at a premium in close-quarter combat in Flanders.

Back in early August 1914, as news of the impending conflict unfolded, Shanghai's Empire Gardens showed a new five-reeler, *The Battle of Gettysburg*. 'Must be seen during the present European War Crisis', cried the advertisement, perhaps more presciently than its opportunistic copywriter knew: the Confederacy failed

ed in England he ran the Cavalry Club at Aldershot.
n many cases, of course, the men were not alone
eir families in joining up; the legacy of the war will
shaped those families for decades to come. William
aby's two brothers were both killed in action.
orn Cleveland Connor, by 1918 a captain in the
ese Labour Corps, died in France two weeks before
ar ended, leaving a one-year-old son. Grimble's
er eventually got both her sons back alive, although
of them was on a disability pension.

me men could not be kept out of the forces.
er HP Evans was discharged from King Edward's
after he was injured by a horse in a stampede.
ning to join the Shanghai Customs in June 1915,
de it back into uniform the following year, joining
oyal Flying Corps. Ernest Engley was invalided
1916, but managed to rejoin as a transport
after a spell back in Shanghai, going on to serve
sopotamia. The deepening conflict scattered the
f Shanghai far across the broken landscape of
e, and to India, the Middle East, and east and
frica. Impatient William Kay, who had diced with
e to get to the enemy more quickly, endured a
ting thirty months as a prisoner of war, during
labour in a German sawmill further damaged
already impaired by a wound sustained at Loos.
Sim was taken during the great German spring

at that battle as it threw thousands of men against artillery, and soldiers manning strongly fortified positions. The soldiers from the south were slaughtered.

By November 1917 Norman Bournes was the only Shanghai policeman left in the 10th Yorkshires. The others were dead, invalided out or had moved to other units, including those able to speak Chinese, who were transferred to the new Chinese Labour Corps. Still, the Shanghai British remained tied together by their letters, their shared memories and the organisations that represented them. The British Women's Work Association sent some 260 000 garments from Shanghai alone by the end of the war, and the China Association sent the men of the Shanghai contingents a Christmas parcel annually. In turn the men diligently wrote their thank-yous on the cards provided.[79] At Shanghai Britons gathered together to mourn men's deaths, as they did for John Douglas in the courtroom beside the British Consulate on 11 January 1916, and this was important, for they felt keenly and personally the losses of those most embedded in the community. But it was equally as important to have these gatherings reported in the press, or obituaries printed, which were then snipped out and sent home to family and friends. They could also gather to hear Major Hilton-Johnson (as he now was) lecture on 'Trench Warfare' at the Union Church Hall, as he returned to take up his old job in the police in May 1916.

The five-score men who sailed west in October 1914 went to do their duty, as they saw it, for God, King and Empire, and to fight for freedom. The irony, of course, is that they did not much reflect on the impaired freedom of China, which provided their livelihoods in Shanghai. They generally saw no contradiction between the war against the German militarism that had directed the violation of Belgium's neutrality, and Britain's own attempt to extend control over Shanghai's northern suburbs but a year earlier. We should not impugn their belief that they rushed home out of a sense of right, but we should remember the nature of the place from which they came.

There were many who were certainly alert to the fact that in the absence of the legions their Chinese 'hosts' might reclaim all that ground lost over the previous seventy years, and who worried that the breakdown of foreign solidarity might send the wrong signals to Chinese nationalists, although they rarely dignified them with that name, preferring to see the threat arising from unruly soldiery or 'Boxers'. In fact, while Chinese entrepreneurs made spectacular inroads into foreign economic predominance during the war and afterwards, the greatest political threat to the European position came from Britain's other East Asian ally: Japan. Leveson, not Fraser, had made the right call. In early 1915 the Japanese presented China with what

became known as the 'Twenty-One Dem[…] attempt to secure a controlling role in variou[…] the Chinese state. Auguries of violence to c[…] seen on the streets of Shanghai in July 1918, [...] clashes between Chinese members of the In[…] Settlement police and Japanese residents.

By the end of the conflict at least sixteen[…] men who had sailed out of Shanghai to[…] echoing off the Bund's fine buildings had[…] fell at Gallipoli, in Belgium and France,[…] Balkans. They died of wounds or sickness[…] Some have graves, some not: George Bra[…] the first day of the Battle of the Somme, a[…] can be found among the 72 000 missing [...] Thiepval Memorial. Alfred Grimble lost h[…] Frank Reuter lost one at Mametz Wood.[…] lost his hearing in one ear. Vaughan Crad[…] Orr, Alfred Scudamore, Frank Stubbings, [...] Thomas Howarth and Allen Cameron we[…] wounded to continue fighting. Stubbings [...] mauled while on night patrol by a grena[…] British sentry who mistook him for a Ge[…] was hit in the face by the tip of a whiz-[…] calibre shell – which 'converted my fac[…] grimly, 'into a penny in the slot arr[…] volunteered for a pioneering operation[…] a part of a shinbone to rebuild his ja[…]

offensive of 1918, and endured seven months of privations and hard labour that saw him drop four stone in weight. He escaped on his third attempt only to die in China four years later, his health still broken. Many of the others who rushed from Shanghai never recovered physically or mentally from the hardships and exactions of the war to end all wars. John Shakeshaft survived it all (though Shanghai thought he was dead), but was killed in action in Egypt in 1942.[80]

Between them these drapers, policemen, lawyers and clerks secured three Distinguished Conduct Medals, seven Military Medals and eleven Military Crosses, mentions in despatches and an OBE. Alfred Grimble tried to stand on his honour with his Distinguished Conduct Medal, initially declining to receive it until awarded by the King in person, but finally accepting it from a lesser representative on 22 August in the gorgeous Chinoiserie surroundings of the Royal Pavilion at Brighton.[81] This was a military hospital for the duration, where he had just had a third operation on his legs, and on a gala day, with the Grenadier Guards Band in attendance, the medal was pinned to his chest. Grimble reported how he was 'overwhelmed with congratulations'. He was phlegmatic about his future, and turned down the offer of renewed employment in Shanghai, notwithstanding that he was 'glad to represent the Far East and Shanghai in particular' at the medal ceremony.

But he now owed it to his mother, 'having got one [son] home as she says alive, from the war even if knocked about a bit', to stay put and not return to Shanghai. 'As, in the fortunes of war I've got knocked about pretty badly and had a rough time, well that risk I took and stand by the consequences without a murmur.'[82]

Grimble was a proud man, and not to be pitied. 'I am like a child learning to walk again,' he wrote in January 1917. Late the following year he reported that 'except for being a bit shorter than I was' – readers might have chuckled grimly at that – 'I am in the pink of condition', and he secured a job with the makers of Brand's A1 sauce. 'His principal regret,' reported police colleague Jim Quayle after looking him up, 'is that he was knocked out so soon and did not get a few more Bosches'. His 'great desire,' another man reported, hitching a line from the popular music-hall song 'Burlington Bertie from Bow', was '"To walk up the Strand"'.[83] Grimble married in 1921, and made sure that Shanghai knew of the birth of his first son in June 1922. He comes through the records as a man who will have taken that walk, head held high.

Shanghai's 'Wounded Soldiers' fund delivered some charity to help tide men through. Robert Orr was given £30 'to set himself up in civilian life again'; Grimble received £40. Orr had been hit while tending to Herbert Such when the latter was shot in the head at Fricourt during the Battle of the Somme, and his arm had to be amputated.[84] Wilcox tried to find relatives of the fallen, not always with success: there were those who had made their way to Shanghai to escape their past, and their roots could not be uncovered.

The war spun many other men out of Shanghai for good. Alfred Scudamore had joked that he was longing to get out of the trenches to the comparative safety of chasing armed robbers in Shanghai, but a revolver accident took him out of the army in 1916, and then out of the SMP.[85] Rowley Evans stayed in the army, but was shot dead in an ambush on India's north-west frontier in 1932. William Martinson also stayed on, serving in Ireland and Palestine. Harold Smeeton returned to policing in Kenya. Ernest Fearn swopped the Shanghai police beat for a newsagent's shop in Bristol. Shanghai had for many always been but one staging post in a career.

Equally as many had made it a home, and so returned, not always immediately. Arthur Chamberlain was wounded in April 1918, his right hand and arm thereafter 'of no use'. Some retraining at a government school for disabled men did not prevent him suffering three years of unemployment before he successfully applied to rejoin the police from a caretaker's job in Birmingham.[86] But some of the Shanghai policemen who took up the jobs that had been held open for them could not readjust. Policeman Thomas Coyne sailed back east with fellow *Suwa Maru* recruit Michael O'Regan, but lasted barely two months back in Shanghai before resigning. O'Regan stuck it only a little longer. When Edward Gladwish and Edward Pilbeam faced dismissal in 1924, their military service led Hilton-Johnson to be lenient with them, and they were allowed to resign instead. Hilton-Johnson knew all too well the pressures of war, and how they persisted. Others, however, stayed on in the force until retirement, like Frank Stubbings, Jim Lovell or William Kay in the 1930s. Another man, Allynne Gimson, would become commissioner of public works in the settlement; Arthur Nugent rose to a senior position in the council's secretariat. War stories surface in obituaries or notes on retirements and departures from Shanghai, or in the occasional article on the British contingent.

German residents in China were expelled in 1919 en masse, which must have come as a relief to some of them, after five years of Sir Everard Fraser's gimlet eye, but the hate and vindictiveness of the war years and of the moment of victory were looked back on with some embarrassment before too long. On 23 November 1918, at the culmination of a three-day carnival that marked the official victory celebrations, Shanghai had paraded caricatures of the Kaiser and leading German generals past the confiscated Club Concordia, hanged them from gibbets at the top of a wooden tower painted with the words 'House of Hohenzollern' – representing the German royal family – and then set them ablaze. French sailors pulled over the *Iltis* memorial a week later. But the Shanghai Rowing Club voted to allow enemy nationals back in 1926, and the German team's missing cups were returned, unharmed. They were gentlemen after all.[87]

A debate on readmitting Germans at one club took place on the anniversary of the *Suwa Maru*'s sailing. An 'ultra patriot' still opposed to the gesture declared that the date alone was moral cause enough to reject it. Up jumped Arthur Nugent to declare he was shortly off to the anniversary dinner, and that he wholly supported letting the Germans back in: the motion was passed.[88] The *Iltis* memorial was quietly re-erected in the grounds of the German school in 1929. Max Hoerter seems to have weathered the storm, dying in Shanghai in 1933, but his children were naturalised as Britons in the 1930s, and after his death his widow regained her British nationality. Sir Everard Fraser died in Shanghai in March 1922, having had a good war; he had worked with British intelligence and the municipal police (it helped having Hilton-Johnson back in charge) to continue to harass and hound German consul general Hubert Knipping.

The *Suwa Maru* continued to ply the route to Shanghai. In May 1932 it brought into Shanghai Captain Bruce Bairnsfather, who had created the most popular of wartime comic characters, the curmudgeonly other-ranker 'Old Bill'. Shanghai presented him with a new war still fresh, suburbs charred after a vicious clash between Japanese and Chinese troops earlier in the year. The ship itself survived until 1943, when, having been requisitioned into military service, it was torpedoed by an American submarine. Such was the usual fate of 'practically unsinkable' ships.

Some sort of social solidarity was performed in Shanghai after the war, to honour the broken and lost lives of the British contingents. A United Services Association was formed in late 1918, but immediately faced criticisms that it was simply a way for the elite to pride themselves on their active charity and their social conscience while ignoring the other ranks of Shanghai. Nonetheless it came to be a fixture of postwar British society locally, disbursing some relief funds for wounded ex-servicemen or others down on their luck. It took a leading role in the lobbying for the construction of the great Shanghai war memorial, designed by Henry Fehr, that was unveiled on 16 February 1924 on the border between the International Settlement and the French Concession. This was accompanied by a gathering of the foreign community on the Bund equalled only in size by that which saw off some of those it commemorated, on the early morning of 16 October 1914. The United Services Association took the main role thereafter in the annual Armistice Day ceremony, held at the memorial, and in the protection of the monument. It helped out too at the funerals of ex-servicemen, acknowledging in the ceremonial of death the contributions men of Shanghai and others who now lived there had made between 1914 and 1918.

The war to end all wars failed to do so, of course. At Versailles, US President Woodrow Wilson's rhetoric of the self-determination of nations had rubbed against the gritty reality of self-interested imperialism. China was not alone in being betrayed at the peace conference, but it was perhaps the most traumatised of those countries ill-treated. The Japanese secured a transfer to themselves of former German interests in Shandong province. As men released from the forces had arrived back in Shanghai in 1919 they found the city, like all of China, galvanised into a great anti-imperialist upsurge that became known as the May Fourth Movement. This would remake Chinese politics and culture, the impact of which resonates still a century later. But socially, at least, the expatriate world looked much the same. And unlike the great wartime changes in Europe, the women of Shanghai had not replaced the men. Instead, shortages of European personnel in the municipal police or the Customs had been solved through recruitment of Japanese. That would become a problem as the years passed by.

Some of the men who sailed would meet annually on 16 October, first doing so in 1923 at Eddie's Café, managed by Ernest Engley. Fourteen got together then, drank and ate well – better than they had done on the ship in 1914 – and each told a tale of their wartime experience. 'Well worth hearing,' commented the *North China Herald*, 'but space forbids.'[89] Space forbids, and so perhaps did the times. Shanghai in 1923 and thereafter had much else to concern itself with. The Germans returned, the Japanese made spectacular gains, and Chinese nationalism started to roll everyone back. Political crises in the 1920s saw the Kuomintang seize power, and the steady erosion thereafter of foreign rights and privileges and that shared 'heritage' on the Huangpu that Shanghailanders tried so hard to preserve in the weird months after July 1914. Still, it remained a good place for those with the savvy to make it work for themselves.

So Shanghailanders old and freshly minted together got down to the business in hand, and the work they were there to do: trying to expand the settlement, creating new engines for generating wealth, and having some fun on the way. They tried out greyhound racing, Basque tennis (jai alai), casinos, corrupt new finance combines, and land speculation. There were massive new mills and other industrial enterprises, and new buildings soared over the Bund. It was business as usual by the Huangpu.

And the clubs, bars, brothels and dancers secured for Shanghai its reputation internationally as 'Sin City', the 'Paradise of Adventurers', the 'Paris of the East'.

War had always been good for business in Shanghai – for somebody's business, somewhere. It made the city, even as it unmade the lives wrecked by the Great War. On Shanghai rolled, into boom years and the occasional bust; cynical, amoral, aware of its debt to the past, but mostly looking forward to opportunities new-provided by each fresh day as it dawned.

DRAMATIS PERSONAE

Suwa Maru contingent

William Douglas Amoss; Ebenezer Auld†; E.W.R. Ayres; Robert Baldwin; Herbert James Beach, M.C.; Charles Edward Beale; Walter Bowden Betts, Med. Mil.; S. Bott; Kenneth Morison Bourne, M.C.; Norman James Bournes, M.M.; George William Bradish†; Arthur Kirkhill Brown, M.C.; Charles Burnie; Francis A. Byrne†; Allen MacArthur Cameron; Arthur John Castle, M.M.; Harold Mayne Catley; Arthur Henry Chamberlain; James Alfred Cheeseman; Frederick William Clifton, M.C.; Alfred John Patrick Coghlan; Cleveland Alexander Connor†, M.M.; William Stanley Cook; Walter Gordon Cope† (joined at Hong Kong); F.C. Corbett; William Basil Cornaby; John Henry Corre; Thomas Graves Coyne; Vaughan Day Kift Craddock; Herbert D. Cranston; William Alexander 'Dolly'

Dalgarno; Theodore Louis Davies; John Charles Edward Douglas†; John Dunbar; Percy St. John Dunckley; Ernest Richard Engley; Ernest Arthur Eva; Tubeville Rowley Evans; H.P. Evans; Ernest Fearn, M.M.; James Frederick Gabbutt; George Eldridge Gilbert, M.C.; Allynne Farmer Gimson; Edward Lovell Gladwish, D.C.M.; Samuel Tidball Glenn; Thomas James Graham; Andrew Thomas Gray; Alfred Frederick Grimble, D.C.M.; Richard K. Hadley; Ralph Noel Heathcote†; Alan Hilton Hilton-Johnson; E. Hope; Thomas James Howarth; Edward Hunt; J.A. Johnson; William White Kay; Bertie Standish 'Kid' Laurence†; James E. Law; Arnold A. Laws; John W. Litt; Archibald Longman, D.C.M.†; Jim F. Lovell, D.C.M.; Thomas Bernard Maguire; William Farrell Martinson; Donald McInnes; Richard Henry Mugford, M.M.; A.R. Murphy; Lewis George Murray Kidd, M.C.; Cecil Albert Nelson; Arthur Gordon Nugent; Thomas Henry Odey†; Michael O'Regan; Robert A. Orr; M.S. O'Sullivan; Sidney Arthur Palk, M.C.; David Palmer; Charles G. Phillips; Percy Oswald Pickburn; Arthur Piercy; Edward Ernest Pilbeam; George Herbert Plumtree; Herbert Edward Pollard†; John Charlot Porter†; Frank Reuter; Jack Reynolds; F.C. Roberts; Harry Summers Robertson; John Ross; Albert Rothery, M.C., M.M.; Walter James Russell; Roy F. Scott, M.C.; Alexander Scougall†; Alfred Allen Vincent Scudamore; John Clifford Shakeshaft;

Martin Hubert Shorto†; William R. Sim; Alfred Richard Singer; Percy Kenneth Sizer; Harold Bruce Smeeton; Charles J. Smith, M.C.; Frank Crofts Stubbings; Herbert Such; Rossiter William Tear; J.W. Thompson; Edward William Trotman; Frederick Osborn Ricks Turner†; Geofrey Aubie Turner; Joseph Twigg-Balmer (joined at Hong Kong); Charles Edward Tyreman (left at Hong Kong); Thomas Stanley Dudley Wade, M.M.; Alfred Wagstaff; W.E. Williams; Edward T. Wilson.

Sources: *NCH*, 24 October 1914, pp. 256–7; *Social Shanghai*, November 1914, pp. 426–31; passenger list: TNA, BT 26/596; enclosure in Shanghai to Peking, No. 136, 17 October 1914, TNA, FO 228/1912.

10th Battalion of the Yorkshire Regiment
Wilfrid Harry Dent†, Arthur De Salis Hadow†, Charles Arthur MacLellan

Shanghai
Heinz Figge; Sir Everard Home Fraser, KCMG; Max Hoerter; Edward Pearce; Annie, Lady de Sausmarez.

ABBREVIATIONS

FO: Foreign Office
NCDN: *North China Daily News*
NCH: *North China Herald*
SHAC: Second Historical Archives of China
SMA: Shanghai Municipal Archives
SMC: Shanghai Municipal Council
SMP: Shanghai Municipal Police
SVC: Shanghai Volunteer Corps
TNA: The National Archives
WO: War Office

SOURCES

Imperial War Museum, London
PP/MCR/195, Col. Arthur De Salis Hadow papers

The National Archives, Kew
FO 228, Foreign Office: Consulates and Legation,
China: General Correspondence, Series I.
FO 371, Foreign Office: Political Departments: General
Correspondence from 1906–1966
FO 917, Foreign Office: Supreme Court, Shanghai,
China: Probate Records.
WO95/2156/2, War Office: First World War and Army
of Occupation War Diaries, 10th Battalion Yorkshire
Regiment, War Diary, 1915 Sept. – 1918 Feb.
WO 363, War Office: Soldiers' Documents, First World
War 'Burnt Documents', surviving records of service for
non commissioned officers and other ranks.
WO 364, War Office: Soldiers' Documents from
Pension Claims, First World War.

Private collection
'Memoirs of Kenneth Morison Bourne'

Second Historical Archives of China, Nanjing
Series, 679, Records of the Inspectorate General of
Maritime Customs

Shanghai Municipal Archives
Archives of the Shanghai Municipal Council

Western Front Association
Army Medal Office. *WWI Medal Index Cards*, via
Ancestry.com

CONTEMPORARY BOOKS
AND JOURNALS

Darwent, Revd CE, *Shanghai A Handbook for travellers
and residents* (Shanghai, 1st edition, 1904)
*Documents Illustrative of the Origin, Development
and Activities of the Chinese Customs Service Vol. III*
(Shanghai, 1938).
Hammond, S. (comp.), *The China War Book . . . – cor-
rected to April 30th, 1916* (Shanghai: CE Sparke
Insurance Office, [1916])

Hammond, S. (comp.), *The Shanghai War Book* (Shanghai: CE Sparke Insurance Office, [1915]).

Minutes of the Shanghai Municipal Council (Shanghai, 2001), 28 vols.

Municipal Council, Shanghai, *Annual Report, and Budget*

North China Daily News

North China Herald

Social Shanghai

War 1914–1918: Record of Services given and Honours attained by of the Chinese Customs Service (Shanghai, 1922)

Wright, Arnold, chief ed., *Twentieth century impressions of Hongkong, Shanghai, and other Treaty Ports of China* (London, 1908)

FURTHER READING

On China's encounter with foreign power in the nineteenth and twentieth centuries see my book *The Scramble for China: Foreign Devils in the Qing Empire, 1832–1914* (London, 2011), and Odd Arne Westad, *Restless Empire: China and the World Since 1750* (London, 2012). Treaty-port social life is nicely caught by Frances Wood, *No Dogs and Not Many Chinese: Treaty Port Life in China, 1843–1943* (London, 1998). On the Shanghai Municipal Police and its men see my *Empire Made Me: An Englishman Adrift in Shanghai* (London, 2003). Eileen P. Scully's *Bargaining with the State from Afar: American Citizenship in Treaty Port China, 1844–1942* (New York, 2001) explores the seedy side of American life in China. For new perspectives on British imperial history see John Darwin, *Unfinished Empire: The Global Expansion of Britain* (London, 2012), and on the impact of the war and Chinese responses to it see Rana Mitter, *A Bitter Revolution: China's Struggle with the Modern World* (Oxford, 2005). Nick Lloyd's *Loos 1915* (Stroud, 2008) provides a compelling account of the battle, and Robert Graves, *Goodbye to all that* (London, 1929) that of a furiously articulate eyewitness. Theatre Workshop's *Oh What A Lovely War* retains its freshness and power.

ACKNOWLEDGEMENTS

In preparing this book I am grateful for advice, hints and research assistance from Alan Crawford, Kate Edwards, Sara Shipway and Alex Thompson, and to Mike Tsang at Penguin for providing the opportunity to dig deep into the history of the 'Shanghai contingent'.

Every effort has been made to trace copyright holders and to obtain their permission for the use of copyright material, but I would be grateful to hear from those we have been unable to trace.

NOTES

1 *North China Herald* (*NCH*), 31 January 1914, p. 310.

2 Jessfield club raid: *NCH*, 28 August 1909, pp. 501–504; 9 October, 92–96; 11 December 1909, 611–616.

3 'Shanghai financial crisis, 1910', in Shanghai to FO, 15 November 1912: TNA, FO 228/2508.

4 Jardine, Matheson & Co., to Consul General, Germany, 22 October 1898, in Consul General to Secretary, Municipal Council, 28 October 1898: SMA, U1-1-716; *NCH*, 28 November 1898, p. 1014.

5 *NCH*, 8 February 1907, pp. 295-6; 'Shanghai Club supplement', *NCH*, 20 February 1909; Arnold Wright, Chief ed., *Twentieth century impressions of Hongkong, Shanghai, and*

other Treaty Ports of China (London, 1908), p. 390.

6   IF Clarke, *Voices Prophesying War: Future Wars, 1763–1984* (Oxford, 1966); Gillian Bickley, *Hong Kong Invaded! A '97 Nightmare* (Hong Kong, 2001).

7   *NCH*, 15 September 1871, pp. 695–7; 29 September 1893, pp. 505–508.

8   *North China Daily News* (*NCDN*), 6 August 1914, p. 10.

9   *NCDN*, 3 August 1914, p. 7.

10 John B. Powell, *My Twenty-Five Years in China* (New York, 1945), p. 55.

11 *NCH*, 8 August 1914, pp. 406-407.

12 Shanghai Tel. No. 190, 1 August 1914: FO 228/1912; Fraser to Jordan, 22 August 1914: FO 228/1911.

13 Police Daily Report, 8 August 1914: SMA, U1-1-1103.

14 *NCH*, 29 August 1914, pp. 661–2.

15 Fraser to Jordan, 6 October 1914: TNA, FO 228/1912.

16 *NCH*, 10 October 1914, p. 94; 'When the first Shanghai British left for war', *NCH*, 14 November 1934, p. 253.

17 Shanghai No. 135, 17 October 1914: TNA, FO 228/1912.

18 Minute of meeting, 7 October 1914, in *Minutes of the Shanghai Municipal Council*

(Shanghai, 2001), Vol. 19, p. 214.

19 Knipping: intercepted letter of 11 November 1914: in Shanghai, undated, to Peking (received 3 December 1914): FO 228/1912. TNA; Unwin: Shanghai Semi-official, c.18 October 1914: SHAC, 679, 32217.

20 Shanghai to Peking, Tel. No. 130, 7 October 1914: TNA, FO 228/1912.

21 Peking to Shanghai, Tel. No. 91, 6 October 1914: TNA, FO 228/1911.

22 *Documents Illustrative of the Origin, Development and Activities of the Chinese Customs Service Vol. III* (Shanghai, 1938), Circular No. 2253, 8 August 1914 (war service), and Circular No. 2255, 10 August 1914 (neutrality mandate), pp. 199–211; Shanghai Semi-official, c.18 October 1914: SHAC, 679, 32217.

23 On these two, and Glenn, below, see Unwin's comments in Shanghai, Semi-official, c.18 October 1914: SHAC, 679(1) 32217.

24 *NCH*, 4 September 1915, p. 688.

25 *NCH*, 17 January 1914, 207.

26 Except where indicated this section is based on reports about the *Suwa Maru* voyage in *NCH*: 31 October 1914, pp. 314, 319, 369; 7 November 1914, p. 436; 14 November 1914, pp. 529, 561–2; 9 January 1915, p. 121; 16 January 1915, pp. 148, 171.

27 *NCH*, 2 June 1928, p. 375.

28 'The Memoirs of Kenneth Morison Bourne', private collection, p. 14.

29 *Straits Times*, 28 October 1914, p. 8.

30 *China Mail*, 21 October 1915; *Straits Times*, 27 October 1914, p. 10.

31 AF Grimble to KJ McEuen, 6 April 1916: SMA, U102-5-23.

32 *NCH*, 9 October 1915, p. 121.

33 *NCH*, 27 February 1915, p. 642.

34 *NCH*, 31 March 1916, pp. 868–9.

35 AF Grimble to KJ McEuen, 6 April 1916: SMA, U102-5-23.

36 *NCH*, 20 Feb 1915, p. 549.

37 Aglen to Wilzer, 14, 23 August 1914: SHAC, 679(1), 32834.

38 Aglen to Taylor, 27 August 1914: SHAC, 679(1), 32834; Peking to Shanghai, No. 206, 21 October 1914, FO 228/1911.

39 Fraser to Jordan, 5 December 1915, confidential: TNA, FO 228/1950.

40 Fraser to Jordan, 30 October 1914: TNA, FO 228/1912.

41 Fraser to Jordan, 22 August 1914: TNA, FO 228/1911.

42 Jordan to Fraser, 24 January 1915: TNA, FO 228/1949.

43 'Prospekt Der Anglo-German Brewery Company, Ltd', 16 April 1903; 'Anglo-German Brewery at Tsingtao': TNA, FO 371/2310/F15722.

44 They all died there: *NCH*, 11 May 1918 p. 348 (Johnston); 5 July 1919, p. 45 (Wrightson); 28 February 1920, p. 550 (Jenner Hogg); 2 May 1925, p. 188 (Prentice).

45 *NCH*, 19 September 1914, pp. 916–28; 26 September 1914, pp. 961, 991–95.

46 *NCH*, 13 May 1915, p. 171.

47 *NCH*, 29 January 1916, p. 254; details on charity work from S. Hammond (comp), *The China War Book*, 2nd edition (Shanghai, 1916).

48 *NCH*, 27 March 1915, pp. 892, 906; *Municipal Gazette*, 14 January 1915, p. 10.

49 On these events and their afterlife see John Horne and Alan Kramer, *German Atrocities, 1914: A History of Denial* (New Haven, 2001).

50 *NCH*, 15 May 1915, pp. 444–5, 464; 22 May 1915, p. 523–4, 540–2; *Municipal Gazette*, 20 May 1915, p. 177.

51 *NCH*, 8 March 1915, pp. 383–390; 15 March 1915, 462–3.

52 Police Daily Report, 12 May 1915: SMA, U1-1-1106.

53 *NCH*, 22 May 1915, p. 524; F. E. Taylor to G.E. Morrison, 14 May 1915, in Lo Hui-min (ed), *The*

Correspondence of G.E. Morrison, vol. II, 1912–1920 (Cambridge, 1978), pp. 399–400.

54 *NCH*, 19 June 1915, pp. 833–4; 14 August 1915, pp. 424–5.

55 *NCH*, 22 May, p. 548. It emerged that he had survived, but was badly wounded – in 17 places: NCH, 12 June 1915, p. 774; TNA, WO 364/3166.

56 Shanghai No. 88, 27 May 1915, including cutting from *NCDN*, 25 May 1915: TNA, FO 228/1949.

57 *NCH*, 7 August 1915, pp. 355–7.

58 See for example Peking Tel. No. 72, 5 June 1915, and Shanghai telegram No. 55, 6 June 1915: TNA, FO 228/1949.

59 Leveson to Canning (China Association), 22 October 1914: SMA, U1-2-0451.

60 *NCDN*, 25 September 1914, p. 7; NCH, 5 December 1914, pp. 74-3; 1 May 1915, p. 319–20; 16 January 1915, p. 178.

61 *NCH*, 20 December 1913, p.902; 27 December, 1913, pp. 955–6; TNA, WO 364/1966. The section following is based on letters published in *NCH*, 20 February 1915, p. 549; 6 March 1915, p. 717; 20 March 1915, p. 869 (Castle); 31 July 1915, p. 310 (Wade); 28 August 1915, p. 578 (Wade); 9 October 1915, p. 117 (FOR Turner).

62 Brigadier-General Sir James Edmonds, Comp., *Military Operations France and Belgium, 1915:*

Battles of Aubers Ridge, Festubert, and Loos (London, 1928), pp. 294–5; NCH, 20 February 1915, p. 549.

63 Letter to Col. ADS Hadow, 22 March 1915: Imperial War Museum [IWM], PP/MCR/195, Papers of Colonel Arthur De Salis Hadow.

64 *NCH*, 23 October 1915, pp. 262–3; Marquis de Ruvigny (comp.), *The Roll of Honour* (London, 1917), vol. 1, p. 321; *NCH*, 16 October 1915, pp. 192–3; 8 January 1916, p. 34.

65 This was Joseph Twigg-Balmer, ex-Customs, who had joined the ship at Hong Kong: TNA, WO 363/B1626.

66 Here and below, except where stated, details of the activities of 10th Battalion Yorkshire Regiment come from the unit's War Diary (TNA, WO 95/2156/2) and from letters in the *North China Herald* (anonymous unless author indicated): 9 October 1915, p. 121 (Dent); 23 October 1915, p. 262 (Castle): 6 November 1915, p. 412 (Bradish), p. 413–4 (Wade); 13 November 1915, pp. 494–5 (Castle); 20 November 1915, pp. 570–572 (G. A. Turner, Hilton-Johnson, Douglas, Craddock); 4 December 1915, pp. 722–3 (Reuter, Such); 24 December 1915, p. 930–931 (Craddock, Palmer).

67 Edmonds, *Military Operations, 1915*, vol. 2, p. 294.

68 Edmonds, *Military Operations, 1915*, vol. 2, p. 344; on the battle see Nick Lloyd, *Loos 1915* (Stroud, 2008).

69 Col. ADS Hadow to Maud Hadow, 26 September 1915; 'Private Diary', 9–23 September, IWM, Hadow papers.

70 AF Grimble to KJ McEuen, 5 March, 6 April 1916, SMA, U102-5-23.

71 *NCH*, 24 November, 1915, pp. 57–1.

72 *NCH*, 9 October 1915, p. 79; *War Memoirs of David Lloyd George Vol. 2.* pp. 67–68.

73 Edmonds, *Military Operations, 1915*, vol. 2, pp. 342, 391–2.

74 *NCH*, 18 December 1915, pp. 865–6.

75 *NCH*, 8 July 1916, p. 54; AF Grimble to KJ McEuen, 6 April 1916, SMA, U102-5-23.

76 On Douglas in this section see *NCH*, 31 December 1915, pp. 995–6, 997; 8 January 1916, p. 70; 15 January 1916, p. 94–5; 12 February 1916, p. 388; probate file in TNA, FO 917/1714.

77 Circulation figure: *NCH*, 3 March 1931, p. 312.

78 *NCH*, 3 November 1917, p. 278; 4 January 1919, p. 23; 30 August 1919, p. 548. Lists of Shanghai casualties can be found in: *NCH*, 2 November 1918, pp. 308–311; 9 November 1918, p. 378; 4 January 1919, p. 23.

79 *Queen Mary's Needlework Guild. Its Work During the Great War. St. James's Palace 1914–1919* (London, [1919]), pp. 77–8.

80 Sim: *NCH*, 21 June 1919, pp. 794–5; Kay: *NCH*,

23 May 1934, p. 267.

81 Grimble's story can be found in his service records: TNA, WO 363/G1142; *NCH*, 30 September 1916, p. 691.

82 AF Grimble to KJ McEuen, 7 July 1917, SMA, U102-5-23.

83 *NCH*, 20 June 1918; 14 April 1917, p. 98.

84 *NCH*, 7 October 1916, p. 51.

85 *NCH*, 8 July 1916, p. 54.

86 AH Chamberlain personnel file: SMA, U102-3-551.

87 *NCH*, 5 April 1919, p. 55; 13 March 1920, p. 700.

88 *NCH*, 1 August 1934, p. 171.

89 *NCH*, 27 October 1923, p. 249.